UNLEASH THE POWER OF PUERILITY

## A DEDICATION TO MY WIFE.

*The book you're holding wouldn't exist*
*without the invaluable encouragement*
*and support of my beautiful, talented,*
*creatively inspiring and very, very, very, very, very, very, very, ve*
*very, very, very, very, very, very, very, very, very, very, very, very, v*
*very, very, very, very, very, very, very, very, very, very, very, ver*
*very, very, very, very, very, very, very, very, very, very, very, very*
*patient wife.* Miss ANNA LONGARETTI.
*......... so if you don't like it, blame her.*

# CONTENTS

INTRODUCTION by

DAVE

TROTT

Whenever I see one of Mark's talks I come out on a high.

High on the possibilities of creativity.

My enthusiasm for what we are supposed to be doing is renewed.

After being told again-and-again all the reasons we can't do anything exciting.

After having the fun sucked out of it in meeting after meeting, I go to hear Mark talk.

And he reminds me that we don't need permission to be creative.

We don't need to wait for planners and account men and clients to suck the life out of what we do.

We can just do it.

If we love an idea, we can find a way to make it happen.

Through friends, half chances, people we meet, we pick up the phone, we call in a favour, or we do someone a favour.

We find other creative people like us who would jump at the opportunity to do something exciting.

And, something that is incredibly rare nowadays, fun.

If we are creative, we can create an opportunity.

That's what Mark's talk reminds me about.

Energy, excitement, risk, and above all, fun.

As soon as I'd seen Mark talk for the first time I went straight back and told my art director, Gordon Smith, that he had to come and see Mark talk.

Like me, Gordon came out high on the possibilities of creativity again.

I told my wife, who's an art director, that she had to see Mark talk.

I told my son, who's a copywriter, and my daughter, who's an art director, that they had to see Mark talk.

They all came out high on the possibilities of creativity.

All reminded of what we'd forgotten: what we should be doing and how we could be doing it.

And we all need reminding.

Somewhere along the way all the marketers and sociologists and semioticians and strategists have sucked all the fun out of advertising.

And along with the fun they've sucked out all the creativity.

Which is exactly what Mark's putting back: fun and creativity.

# MY BIT UP THE FRONT!

**Now, I know what you're thinking: Mark's been working since before I was born and he's the proud owner of a Transport For London Bus Pass, so how does that make him puerile? There's a simple answer to that: I was born puerile. So were you. So was everyone. Most people grow out of it but it dawned on me only recently that, intellectually, my ideas haven't matured much since I was at primary school. Yet here I am, in a young person's business, surviving - no, thriving - by still doing what I love. And that's totally down to the *Power of Puerility*. I was called 'puerile' at school, by my teacher Mr. Bentley, in Form 4a. I didn't know what it meant at the time but, as it turns out, for a successful career in advertising there is no greater compliment. I spent most of my formative years watching cartoons, reading any comic I could get my hands on and drawing. This meant, by the time I left school, I had very few qualifications and even fewer prospects. Being 'a bit arty' I didn't really fancy a career**

CHAS
NELL
TURBO
TURKISH DISGUST
STRANGE SENSATION
NUT SUPRISE
BOMBE CLUSTER
SALT & VINEGAR
HEART de BERNE

working in my old man's South London scrapyard and getting dirt under my fingernails. I wanted to do other things with my hands like hairdressing. Or window displays. My mum made a good suggestion. "Mark, you can draw a bit," she said, "Why don't you become one of those painters who paints the patterns on crockery?" It was only the fact that I didn't have any mates in Stoke-on-Trent that put me off. But there I was, fresh out of school with nothing but a quiff (yes really) and a scooter to my name (a Lambretta SX 200, since you ask). I was outside my house polishing it one day, when an odd-looking bloke with a head like a wasp (Hello, Duncan) pulled up on his moped to admire it. The conversation moved from scootering to scribbling. He said he was on his way to the Ravensbourne School of Vocational Studies, which was a bit like art school only you didn't need as many O Levels to get in. I rushed indoors, went upstairs, counted mine and found I had the requisite three. I signed

**up the very next day. There followed a couple of fun-filled years learning about typography, photography, screen-printing and architectural drawing, before landing a job as a visualiser at Leo Burnett - a massive advertising agency on St. Martin's Lane in London. Armed with a layout pad and a full set of Magic Markers, my job was to draw up various art directors' press and poster concepts and storyboards. Of course, (you're way ahead of me, aren't you?) it wasn't long before I fancied becoming an art director myself. I thought it would be much more fun to scamp up my own ideas instead of other people's. My boss at the time, Norman, was an active member of the '11:01 Club'. He'd disappear to the pub at 11:01 to prop up the bar 'til chucking-out time just after three. I was left behind to answer his phone. If it was a photographer's rep or a producer, wanting to show a portfolio or reel I'd pretend it was my office and that I was the art director. I took the liberty of pulling out my own drawings and**

REJECT
OLD
SNEAK

OLD
OLD
OLD
OLD
OLD
OLD
OLD
OLD
OLD

ideas, then I persuaded those good people to shoot them. That's when I learnt a valuable lesson: always answer the phone. You never know who, or what sort of opportunity, might be on the other end of the line. Having amassed a portfolio filled with ideas, I answered the phone one day and it was a talented young copywriter by the name of Chris Palmer. He was calling from Bartle Bogle Hegarty, one of London's hottest new advertising agencies, to offer me a proper job as his art director. A couple of years later, I answered the phone again. This time it was Lowe Howard-Spink. They were an even bigger agency and they were offering Chris and me an even bigger job. We got to work for great clients like Heineken, Ovaltine and Parker Pens, but we felt like we'd *really* made it when we were briefed to come up with a campaign to launch the new Vauxhall Cavalier. It was going to be the UK's biggest ever car launch and it was all going swimmingly. However, one day, on a whim, we decided to give up our big jobs and handsome salaries. We thought it might be a laugh to plunge ourselves into poverty by setting up our own agency - Simons Palmer DENTON Clemmow and Johnson. I didn't really appreciate it at the time, but as an agency we were bloody good (he said modestly). Of course, it helped that we surrounded ourselves with some of the hungriest and most talented creatives in town, along with an account team (headed up by Carl Johnson) that could sell any creative ideas we came up with, no matter how outlandish. Our agency won shedloads of awards for clients like Nike, Wrangler, Greenpeace, BT and Terence Higgins Trust. We were riding high but, unfortunately, politics got in the way of creativity and Chris and I were ousted from the place we founded. The experience had left me a bit shell-shocked so, as a stop-gap, I thought I'd have a bash at directing TV commercials until I worked out what to do next. To my absolute amazement, I'm still doing it today - over twenty-five years later. That and

**designing, drawing silly pictures, working with great photographers and a whole host of other stuff. Like giving my talks. I never planned to launch myself on to the lecture circuit; the talks sort of happened by accident. In fact, before unforeseen circumstances compelled me to do it, the idea of public speaking would have me breaking out in a cold sweat. Initially, to get over my nerves, I thought the best approach would be to just stand up in front of an audience and share some of my creative stories, as though I was chatting to a few mates. In my head, I replaced the word 'scared' with 'excited', and found I was enjoying being on stage. The audiences must have enjoyed it too, because I kept getting invitations to do more. Not only from advertising agencies, but also from clients I'd never heard of in places I'd never even been. So where does the Power of Puerility come in? (I hear you ask). After giving more than a hundred talks, I've realised that no matter how different my self-initiated**

**creative projects are, they all tend to follow a similar pattern: HAVE AN IDEA THAT COULD BE THOUGHT UP BY A SCHOOLBOY (Or for that matter, a schoolgirl. The definition of puerile isn't "boyish" but "childish", puerility is gender-neutral). INVEST IN IT. And by that, I don't just mean money. HAVE A PISS-UP AFTERWARDS. Whatever the outcome, it's very important to celebrate giving birth to a new creative entity. WAIT FOR A MAGICAL, UNEXPECTED RESULT. Sometimes a financial return, but often, something much, much better. And that, my friends, is the *Power of Puerility* in a nutshell. Use it wisely and never, ever for evil. Now sit back and enjoy a rollercoaster ride of stories that will both illustrate and prove my theory. Some were proper commercial ventures but many were non-commercial *ad*ventures: examples of "*Why don't we.....?*" made real. Just remember two things: 1. In life, it's easier to get forgiveness than ask permission. 2. Please keep your arms and legs inside the ride at all times.**

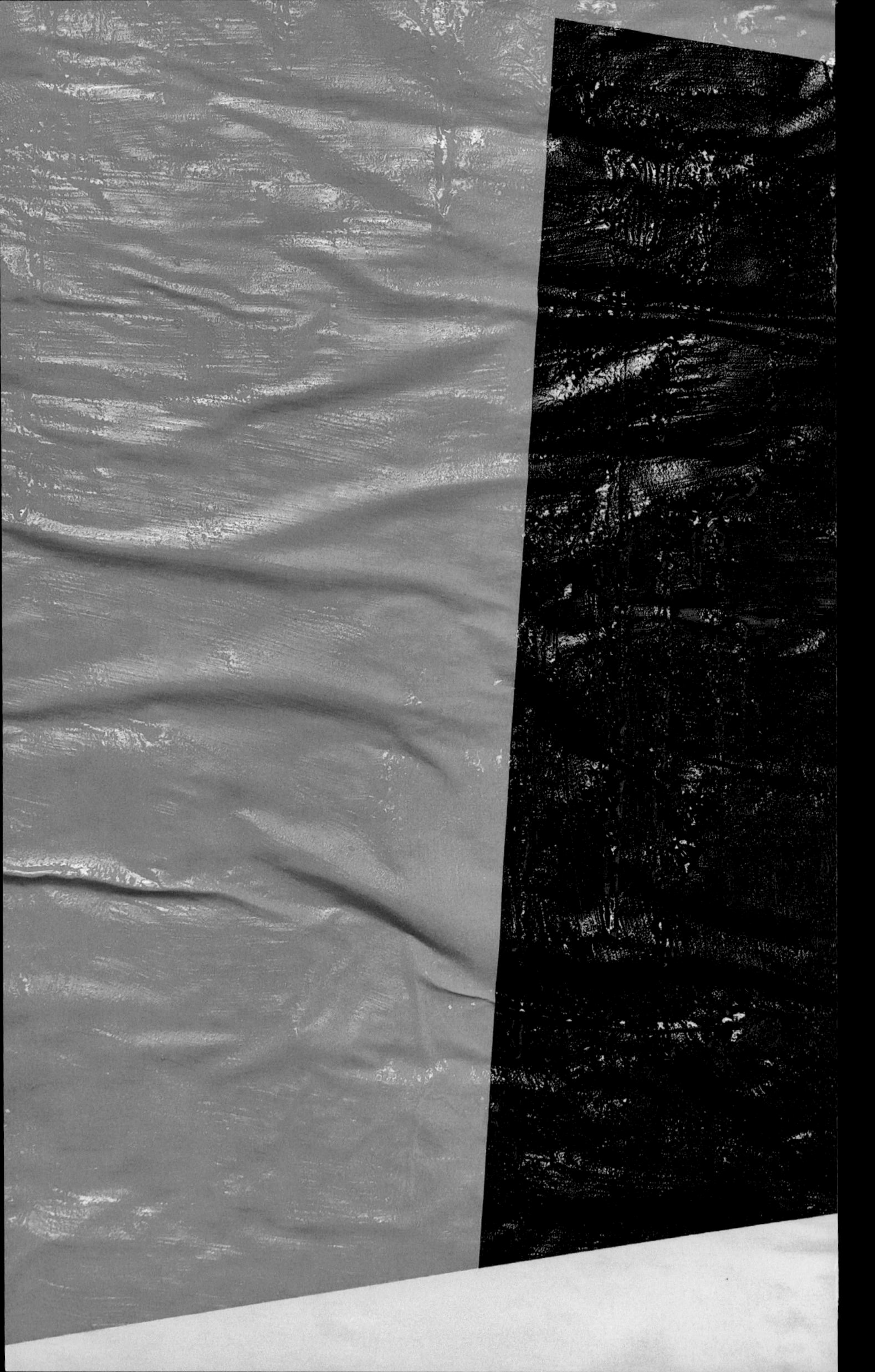

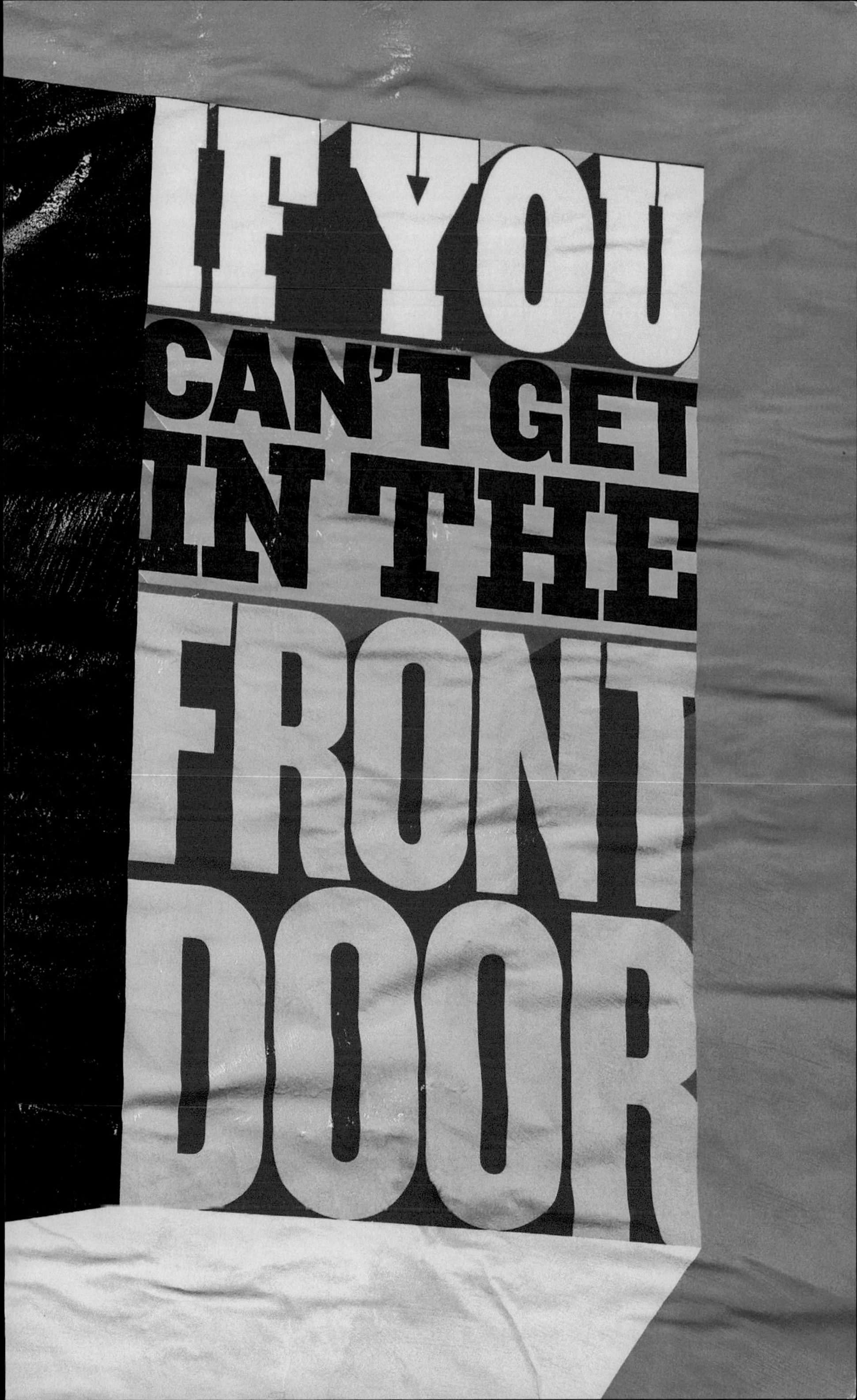

IF YOU
CAN'T GET
IN THE
FRONT
DOOR

**In 2008, I decided to set up a new production company. Brimming with optimism after a fantastic stint at Therapy Films, I wanted to start a new venture with my name above the door. Actually, that's not quite true. I wanted my name above the door figuratively but not literally. So what was I going to call this exciting new company? You may find this hard to believe but up to this point I'd always been quite bashful. Almost (I said almost) self-effacing, preferring to let my work do the talking. Maybe it was time for a change... time to stop being modest and start showing off - BIG TIME! Though - just to be contrary - I was going to call this new, showy-offy venture, 'Modesty'. I excitedly shared my thoughts with my new partner (and producer) Sara Cummins, and she loved the idea. After a bit of research, I was disappointed to discover a production company called Modesty Films already existed. So I whipped out my thesaurus and right there, under the word 'modest', was 'coy'. That sounded pretty good to me. But to make 'coy' a**

TRY
GOING
ROUND
THE
BACK

HOW TO
SURVIVE 33¾
YEARS IN
ADVERTISING
The ramblings
of M.Denton Esq.
at RKCR/Y&R,
Thurs, 14th July,
from 5pm til ???

little less coy, I wrote it in caps and added a screamer. Thus, 'COY! Communications' was born. I designed a strikingly immodest identity, rented a swanky suite of offices and sat back, waiting for the phone to ring. And I waited. And waited. Nothing. So we stood by the fax machine: zilch. About seven minutes and fourteen seconds after we moved in, the global financial crash smashed into the advertising industry and our flashy new offices were eerily silent. Our rep couldn't get her toe in the door, let alone an appointment to present the showreel. Having no work to offer, agencies had pulled up the drawbridge, leaving us shivering on the other side of the moat. I was hearing the same story from other production companies. Usually just before they went out of business. I urgently needed to raise awareness of COY! This was no time to be...well... *coy*. Instead of our rep hoping for a dinky 10-minute meeting, what if I ignored the usual way of doing things, like making appointments and all that malarky and just went in and gave a talk? That would mean I'd have a captive audience of creatives and producers for a whole hour. So, when I was planning out the talks, I decided that I wasn't going to give it the hard sell. If advertising has taught me anything it's that if you want people to buy, sometimes it's best not to 'sell'. I didn't even play them the company showreel. In fact, I only played one commercial and it wasn't one of mine. It was a black & white advert showcasing the Johnny Seven OMA (One Man Army): the best-selling toy of 1964. It was a big plastic gun that incorporated seven deadly weapons in one. As a seven-year old child with a penchant for weapons of mass-destruction it was the first advert that really affected me. And so I made that the basis of the talk and I hoped to inspire people who heard it. It must have had an effect, because there was a direct correlation between me giving a talk at an agency, and a script from that very agency chut-chut-chuttering out of the fax machine. The more talks I gave, the

**more I enjoyed doing them. And I can only presume that other people enjoyed them too, because I'm happy to report that I'm still getting requests. I suppose it became, as these things often do, a self-fuelling machine. Although the basic premise of every talk was essentially the same, I invited any agency that booked me to come up with a poster for it. That served two purposes. It gave the agency in question some skin in the game and a different range of posters implied that I gave different talks. One poster was particularly well received: It was created by The Partners (now Superunion) and involved having my bald dome beautifully painted by the artist Vic Lee. You can see why it won a big clutch of awards. Though I try not to let this striking image of my head go to my head. All the posters worked brilliantly: I didn't have to 'sell' myself to the agencies, the agencies proved only too happy to sell me to themselves. So my advice is, if you ever find you can't get in the front door, try going round the back.**

INSIDE THE MIND OF

# MARK DENTON

5TH JULY, 6:30PM, PARTNERS' PARTNERS TALK

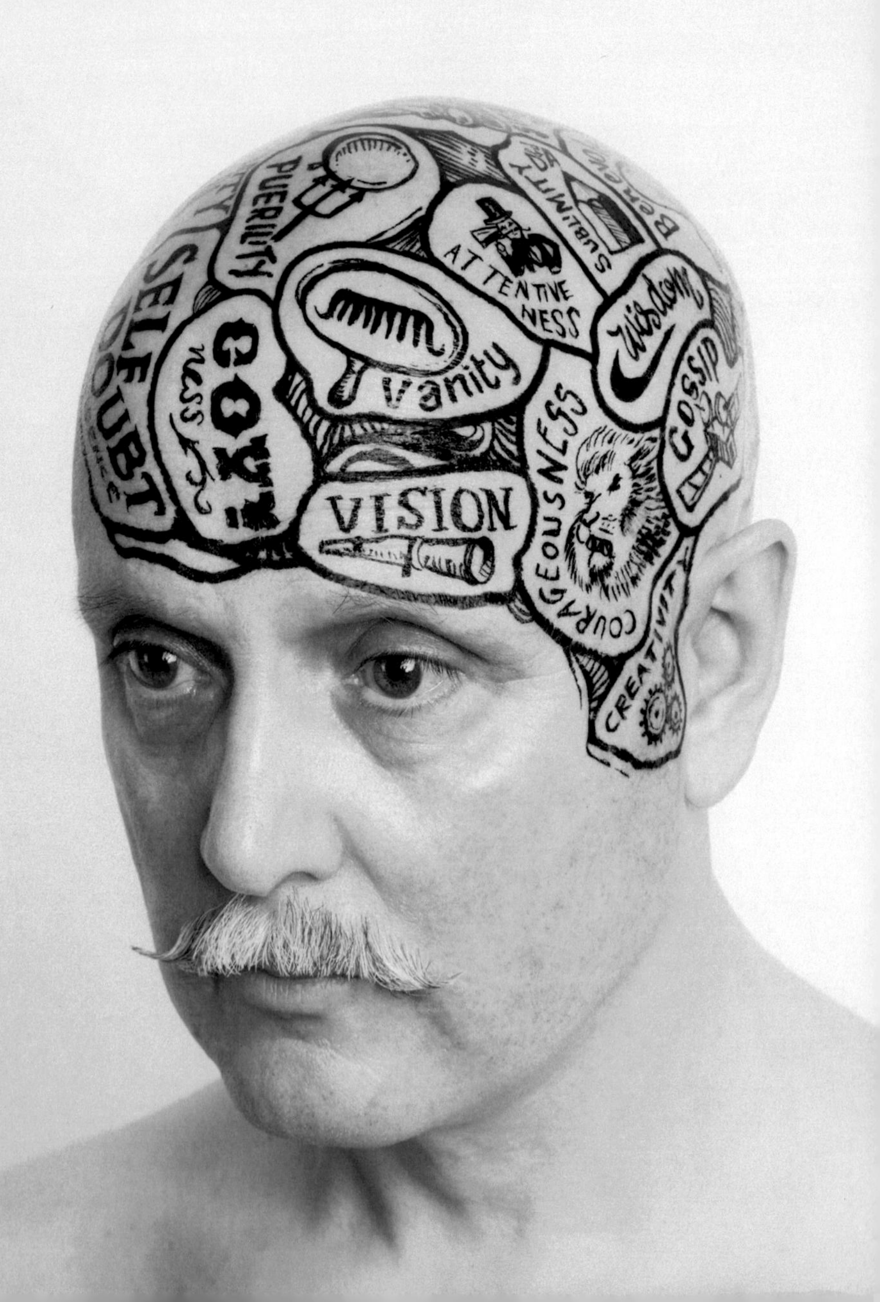

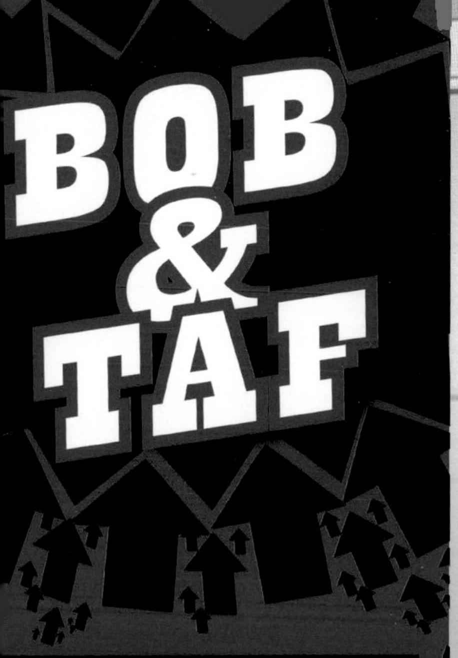

BOB
&
TAF
Will be attending a talk on blatant self promotion
by Mark Denton
OgilvyOne Creative Department 4.30 Jan 30th


MARK DENTON TALK
5PM
IRIS

COUNSELLING SESSION
6PM
'YOU ARE NOT A FAILURE'

BASTARD
SANTA
A SAD STORY BY
LITTLE MARKY DENTON
(ESQ)
2:15PM * SEPT 19TH * KINSALE SHARKS

YOU CAN'T SHUT HIM UP
C4 INSPIRATION TALKS | THURS 5PM | THE CINEMA

PUBLICITY
SHY
TALK BY MARK DENTON ESQUIRE AT SHOREDITCH TOWN HALL WEDNESDAY 22ND JANUARY

MARK DENTON SHOWS OFF HIS RATHER MAGNIFICENT BODY OF

OgilvyOne, 30th Jan, 4.30pm

Yes.

K DENTON ESQ TALKS • MEDIA ARTS LAB • FRIDAY 4TH NOVEMBER • 11AM

HELLO
my name is
Mark
AWARENESSNESSNESS
a loud talk by mark denton esq.

# DENTON

## ON CREATIVITY. ON ADVERTISING. ON LIFE

5th Feb 6pm, St Luke's

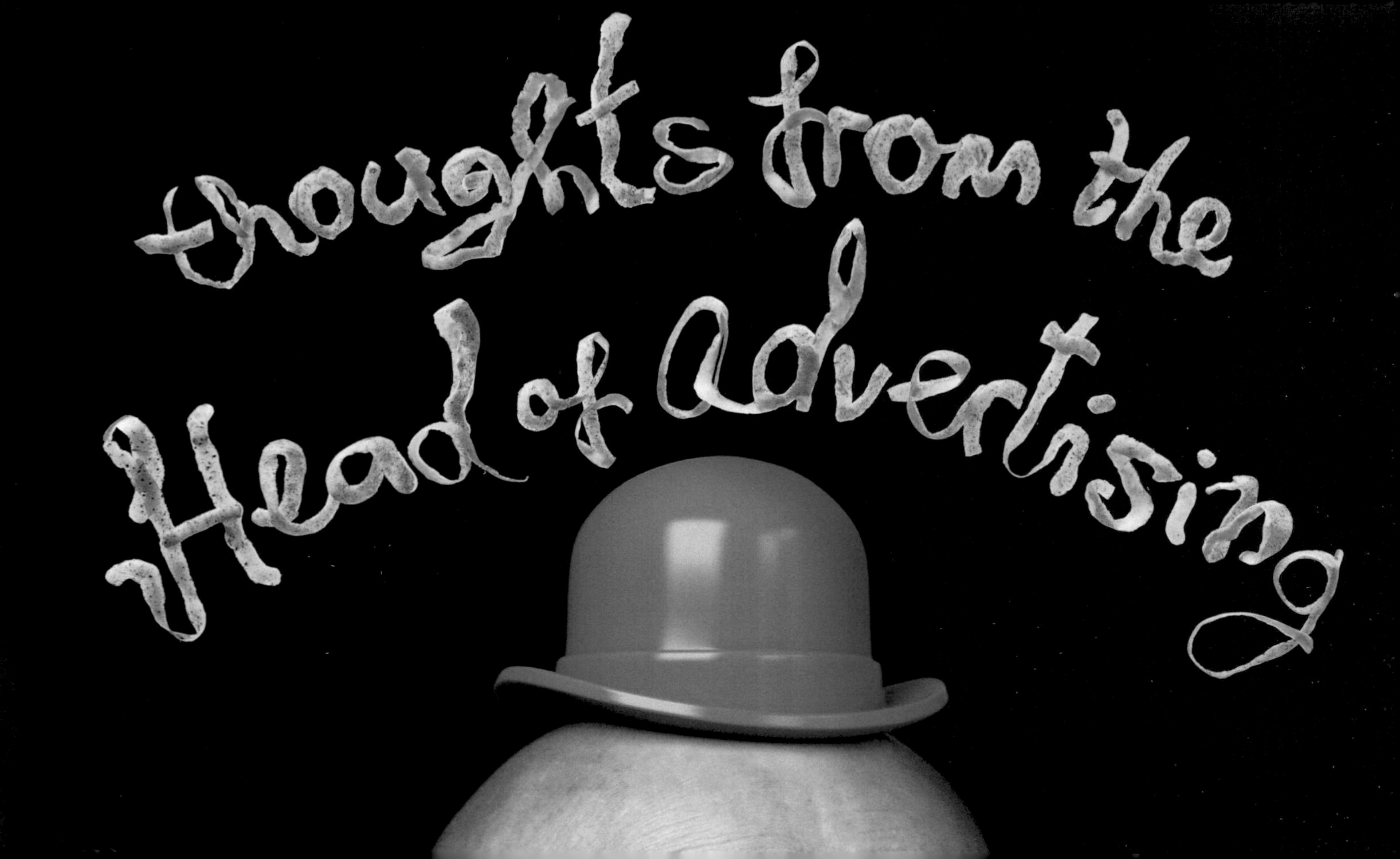
thoughts from the
Head of Advertising

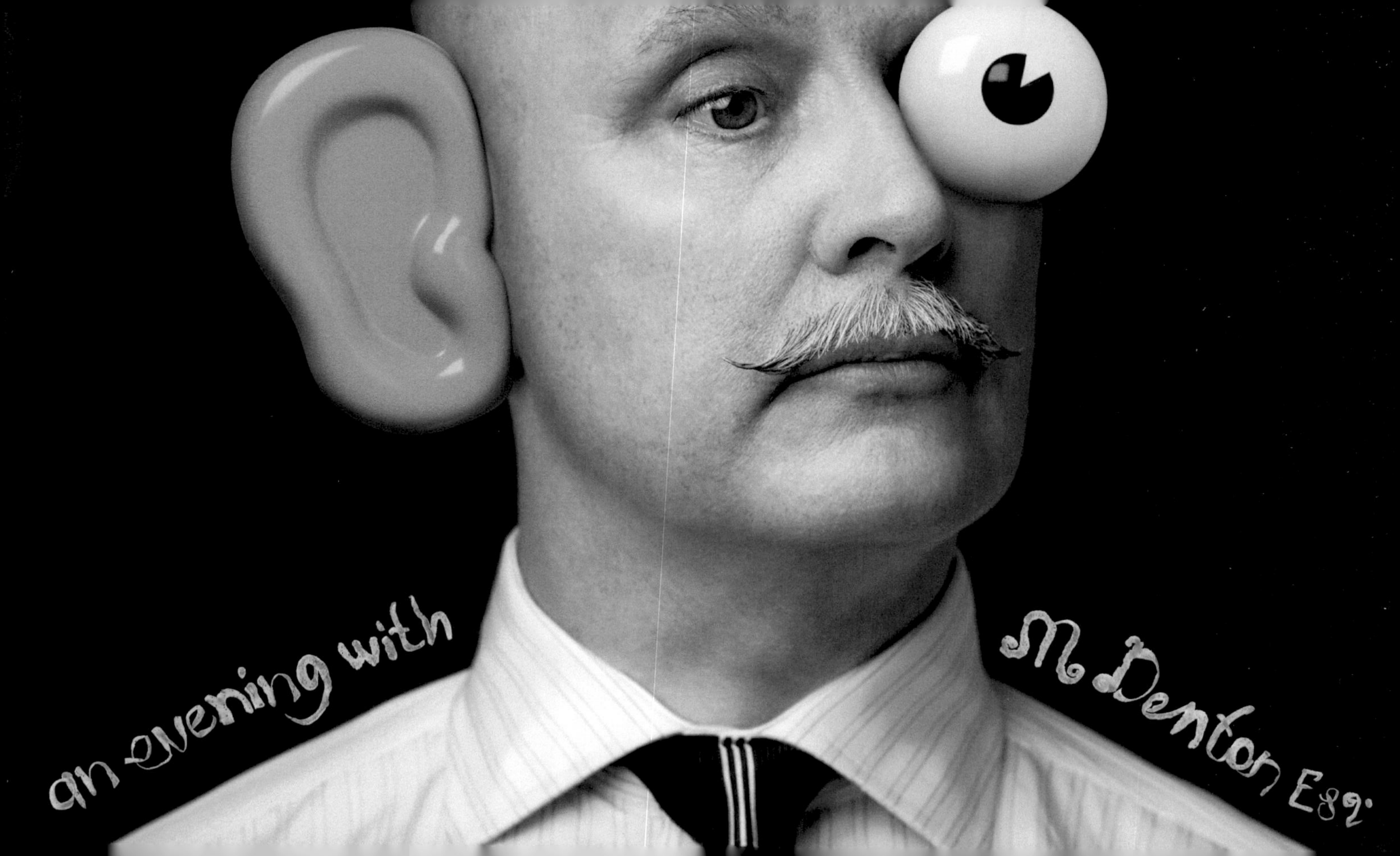
an evening with
Mr Denton Esq.

LIVE SHOW

180 Amsterdam asked if I minded dressing up in a ladies nightie. What they didn't realise was they were pushing against an open door...

THE CLIENT
DOESN'T
DO IT

ANT IT
WAY!!

**Back in the 80s, I owned a slice of an advertising agency and my job was to provide the creative stuff. Among our early clients was Wrangler. Their once-iconic jeans had fallen way behind Levi's: undoubtedly because of one of the most successful TV advertising campaigns of all time. These famous commercials featured Levi's 501s on (and off) some of the most gorgeous people in the world. So Levi's were far-and-away the best-selling jeans on the market, Pepe were second, and Wrangler were (a distant) third. Desperate to re-capture their former glory, Wrangler hired us with the brief; 'Do something better than Levi's'. So no pressure then. We talked to their target audience (aged 15-25), who thought Wranglers were pretty lame, especially that 'W' stitched onto the back pocket. So they suggested we shouldn't feature the 'W' too prominently in the ads. Hmm. Thing is, my inclination has always been to run towards a problem rather than away from it. I felt compelled to make the 'W' the star of the show. So our new commercial centred on the letter 'W' with a clever**

Wrangler

BE MORE THAN JUST A NUMBER

(well I thought it was a bit clever) endline: *'Be More Than Just a Number'.* It was perfect, because it suggested that a letter (W) was better than a number (501). Just because something's a good idea doesn't stop me trying to think of other ways to make it even better. Legal or otherwise. In the 1980s, it wasn't *strictly* legal to put up fly posters and, despite threats, 'Bill Stickers'-whoever he was-was rarely prosecuted. Fly posters were a common sight; usually promoting gigs, singles or albums. Aimed primarily at teenagers, they were always eye-catching, usually with bold type and colourful visuals. It struck me that Wrangler could do the same; by creating big, bold versions of the letter 'W' with *'Be More Than Just a Number'* underneath, then plastering them on top of those music posters: exactly where the target audience would be looking. After that, we could generate a sassy bit of publicity to back up the TV campaign. So I scamped up some fly posters and showed them to the client. He responded to 'W' with two letters of his own - 'N' and 'O'. "Just get on with the film." he said. I was a bit miffed because I thought they'd be really effective but, with a heavy sigh, I put them aside and did as he asked. Then the phone rang: it was a young photographer called Malcolm Venville (write that name down, it'll come up later). He wanted to show me his portfolio, and I was more than happy to look at it. It was good. Very good. And, better still, he agreed to shoot those fly posters the client had rejected. I explained that they were unlikely to run but, since he liked my idea as much as I liked his portfolio, he was willing to take a chance. We had great fun shooting them, and in the next client meeting I said; "Remember those 'W' fly posters?" "Yes," he replied, "but please don't mention them again: I told you, we don't want them". So I didn't mention them again. I just placed them silently on the table in front of him: finished and fabulous. "Ah," he said, "I didn't realise they'd be this good. Do they have to be fly posters?" They ran instead as proper 4 and 6-sheet posters - as press ads, and were printed on T-shirts that sold by the truckload alongside the jeans. So remember, now and again 'N-O' spells 'Yes'.

I DIDN'T REALISE THEY'

OOK THAT GOOD!

**BAD BARNET, GOOD IDEA. I was asked to direct a lovely commercial for 'Brylcreem', (the world renowned range of hair products) set in a fictitious place called 'Bad Barnet' where everyone from the Mayor to the Police Chief's dog, had an appalling hair-do. I loved this idea and designed everything in and around the town of Bad Barnet: election posters for Daniel Druff a mayoral candidate with a terrible mop top; adverts for rival products like '*Hair Lube*', '*Styling Lard*' and '*Quiffy*'; and a complete local**

**newspaper called '*The Bad Barnet Bugle*'. I know. I'd only been asked to shoot a television commercial but I'd gone off and produced an actual newspaper. It was just a prop - on screen for no longer than $1\frac{1}{2}$ seconds - but I couldn't help myself. I'd made a whole newspaper - complete with articles, pictures and press advertising - from scratch. Then I wrote what is probably still my best line ever; 'EXPLOSION IN WIG FACTORY. POLICE COMBING THE AREA!' and splashed it across the front page. I shot the**

Welcome to BAD BARNET, where

when they're applying a LARG

ne locals are never happier than

ollop of grease to a duck's ass...

**commercial and everyone was delighted but I couldn't help thinking that 'The Bad Barnet Bugle' deserved a bigger readership. Perhaps it would make a fantastic sales presenter for Brylcreem? I re-jigged the design a bit and presented it to the client. He loved it but balked at the cost of printing it. I asked if he'd mind if I went ahead and published it anyway? "Not at all," he said, "Go ahead." So I went ahead and re-re-jigged it again, this time into a promotional piece for Mark Denton Esq. It generated a load of**

**publicity and went on to win quite a few awards. To my surprise it was even featured in an architectural magazine. The journalist wrote, "We don't know why we've been sent this but we really like it." That's why I always send out stuff to random magazines and unlikely famous personalities. Why wouldn't you? I once sent something to Sir Paul Smith and he returned the compliment with a beautiful pair of socks. Mind you, I'm still waiting to hear back from Marlon Brando. What's that? He died in 2004? Oh.**

By Bob Short
Styling
LARD
EXTRA FIRM HOLD
ISSUE #1
EXPLOSION
POLICE COMB
POLICE were called to the outskirts of Bad Barnet in the early hours of the morning to
Local Boy Discovers The Da
Of Messing With Beehives
By Bob Short
A TEN-YEAR old s
boy had his bottom
today, following a silly p
with a Beehive. The bo
said to have fired a w
pistol at it, thus angering
Beehives owner, teac
Miss.Barber. "It takes
over 2 hours a day not
FOR QUIFFS
IN A JIFFY...
Town Hall
See SIDEBOARD, page 5
a stray mu
TOWNSFOLK were in
Critics and public alik
bbers
Haire
ES, WE S
rpin
Crash

arnet Bugle

LOOK - SERIOUSLY BAD HAIR DAY

LATE EDITION

PRICE 60¢

IN WIG FACTORY

RING THE AREA

WIG FACTORY

G THE AREA

PRISON SENTENCE FOR RAZOR GANG

B. COUNTY POLICE DEPT

8 5136 1940 7

NOTORIOUS gang themselves behind earlier today. The Judge who sentenced them said They used to hang around in

gang behind The Judge them said around in

NOTORI themse earlier toda sentence hey used to h

TOU MANUFA INVO IN M

Style #72 - THE 'DIPLOMAT'
BAD BARNET
RUG RAKE
ONLY!
$1 50
Style #84 - 'HIAWATHA'
Style #19 - THE 'DEBONHAIR'
NEW!
LOBE
'LOPPER'
Only $5 plus tax
Style #2 - 'WOODY'
Bad Barnet
Boncé
POMADE
TERMS COD
$15 — 00
$10 — 00
PAID
Style #403 - 'MAVERICK'
HAIR LUBE
PHOTOS BY

Style #328 - THE 'HIGH-BROW'
Style #85 - 'LOWAWATHA'
Style #87 - 'EL GRANDE'
Style #105 - 'BOMBHEAD'
Style #106 - THE 'POLECAT'
Style #107 - THE 'SKYLINE
Style #108 - THE 'DIRECT
Style #109 - THE 'TURTL
Style #110 - THE 'SOP
Style #111 - THE 'BIC
Style #112 - THE 'DO
Style #113 - THE 'K
Style #114 - THE '
Style #115 - 'PU
Style #116 - 'T
Style #117 - T
Style #118 -
FOR QUIFFS
IN A JIFFY...
day, following a silly prank
with a Beehive. The boy is
said to have fired a water
pistol at it, thus angering the
Beehives owner, teacher
Miss.Barber. "It takes me
over 2 hours a day not to
Town Hall to An

CAUTION: avoid prolonge

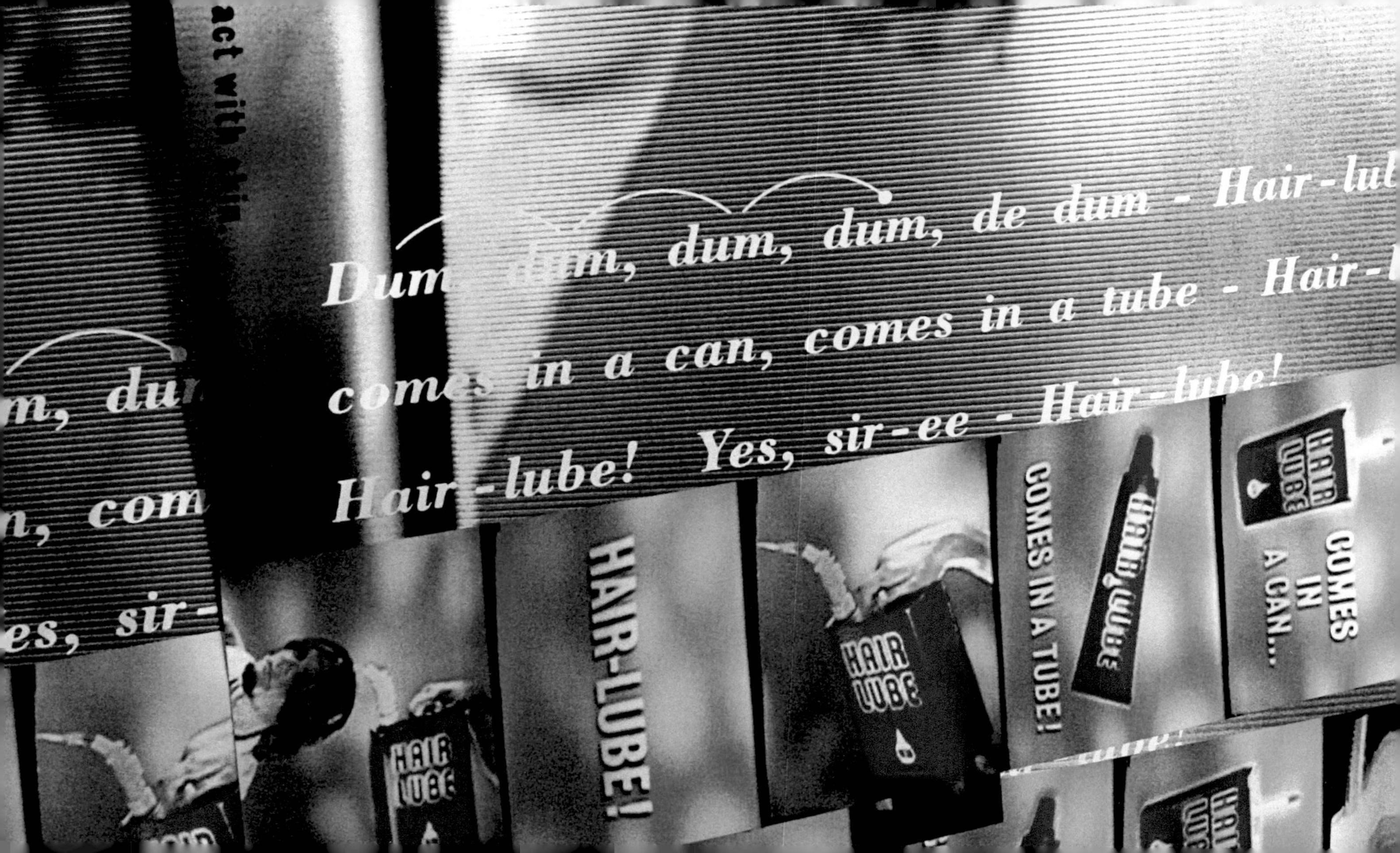
Dum, dum, dum, dum, de dum - Hair-lu
comes in a can, comes in a tube - Hair-
Hair-lube! Yes, sir-ee - Hair-lube!
act with
COMES IN A CAN...
COMES IN A TUBE!
HAIR-LUBE!
HAIR LUBE

YOU ARE NOW LEAVING
BAD BARN

IT'S BETTER T

DO

THAN

DO IT!

**You know those moments when you're down the pub and someone has a daft idea: you all laugh, you get another round in, and the daft idea is never mentioned again? Funnily enough, I don't. You see, when I have a daft idea, I also have an immediate compulsion to make it happen. Because one of my many mottos is 'It's better to do it than not do it.' For example, a few years back, I was on a photographic shoot with Malcolm Venville when I suddenly got the urge to dress up as my fictional forebears. So, naturally, the first thing I did was to turn to Malcolm and say, "How do you fancy taking some photos of me, dressed up as my ancestors?" Malcolm is another firm believer in 'It's better to do it than not do it'. So a few days later, there I was: posing in front of his camera as 'The Very Reverend Pious Smallpiece (Bishop of Chalfont St Giles)', 'Walter Fortescue Denton the Younger', 'Fireguard the Fearless', 'Tarquin Incapability Denton' and an assortment of others. It was great fun - the archetypal 'stupid idea'- though**

SPANK

neither of us gave much thought to why we were there or what we'd do with the pictures once they were finished. The last ancestor we photographed was '*Nobby Bottomshuffle*', an Edwardian footballer. 'Nobby' was me dressed in ridiculously long shorts, arms folded, with my foot on an old-fashioned leather ball. Chris, my creative partner and an ardent Spurs fan, had come along to the shoot. As soon as he saw Nobby, he suddenly reverted to the behaviour he'd been displaying for years at White Hart Lane. "Free kick!" he yelled from the sidelines. "Now take a throw-in! How about a sliding tackle?" When we got the photos back, they were funny. Really funny. Chris said he hadn't laughed so much since the last time Arsenal missed a penalty. We had to do something with them but what? I looked at 'Nobby' again and remembered the collection of old cigarette cards that my grandad had given to me when I was a nipper. On the front of each one was an image of a player, demonstrating a particular move

IT'S A FUN
GAM
THE GENTLEMA
ASSOCIATION

OLD
UIDE TO
BALL

and on the back were instructions on the best way to execute it. That was it! Nobby Bottomshuffle was to star in his own set of cigarette cards: *It's a Funny Old Game*, courtesy of *Coffmore Cigarettes* [Now with Added Tar] I designed them, Chris wrote the instructions and I printed an album to put them in. Lovely Fun project. Full stop. Or so I thought Walking down Charlotte Street one day, I noticed an empty shop with an estate agent's board in the window. It looked a bit like an art gallery. Back then, no-one had ever heard the phrase 'pop-up shop' but, as I gazed through the glass, I could see a pop-up-opportunity Out came the phone, and a quick call to the agent secured the space for a week. It was re-christened 'Sproteville Gallery' for the next seven days and we transformed it into the Nobby Bottomshuffle exhibition. Further phone calls resulted in us getting fish & chips and beer for free. But best of all, an offer to turn those little cigarette cards into 8 x 4 foot prints. My mate

Ron Mueck, sculpted and cast three busts of Nobby to create an old-fashioned shop display promoting, '*Tuff Sheet - Non Absorbent Toilet Tissue*'. Finally Steve Smithwick, ace production designer, added a final flourish with things like hand-painted concrete footballs and stuffed team mascots. There was only one thing left to do: invite 400 luminaries of the British advertising industry and have a knees-up. It was a fantastic night and a fitting *finale* to such a fun project. Or so I thought. About a week later, the phone rang. And as you now know I always pick it up... It was the famous designer Ben Casey from the equally-famous design company, The Chase. He explained that a friend of his had gone on and on about our little exhibition and, since he'd just designed the new National Football Museum in Preston, would Nobby like to go on display there? We could even sell the cigarette card albums in the gift shop. I said I'd speak to Nobby and, sure enough Nobby said he'd be honoured. After that, Ben only went and asked me if I'd like to direct a commercial for the National Football Museum too. As they say in football, I was 'absolutely over the moon' and, just as I was coming back down to earth, the phone rang again. This time round it was Dave Waters, from one of London's most creative advertising agencies, Duckworth Finn Grubb Waters. One of his creative teams had written a TV commercial featuring a famous footballer eating a Müller Fruit Corner, while taking a corner. Trouble was, the budget wouldn't stretch to a famous footballer so how did I feel about not only directing the ad, but also starring in it as Nobby Bottomshuffle? Do I really need to tell you how I felt about such a lovely offer? So, an even *more* fitting finale to a fun project. Now, I know what you're thinking, Nobby Bottomshuffle this, Nobby Bottomshuffle that... what about all the other fictional ancestors? What a complete waste of time they turned out to be

(*Hold that thought until you get to page 86*)

COFFMORE CIGARETTES
THE LONG THROW IN
IT'S A FUNNY OLD GAME
THE GENTLEMAN'S GUIDE TO ASSOCIATION FOOTBALL
9
The Early Bath.
Should unfortunate circumstances befall the Association Footballer, namely upon the occasion of a premature dismissal, he must always endeavour to act with a degree of dignity that befits a sportsman. Accept your fate like a man, upper lip as stiff as humanly possible and console yourself in a 'Coffmore'. The ideal companion when dealing with death in the family, local pit disast or sporting tragedy such as be sent off for impailing your stu an opponents' sweetbreads. Life a seems better with a 'Coffmore' - now with added Tar!
ISSUED BY
COFFMORE & SONS
COFFMORE CIGARETTES
RECEIVING A KNOCK

IT'S A FUNNY OLD GAME
THE GENTLEMAN'S GUIDE TO ASSOCIATION FOOTBALL
10
The Sliding Tackle.
The sliding tackle is one of the hallmarks of the English game. It is particularly effective during the winter when weeks of suicidally depressing drizzle have rendered the pitch a heaving quagmire. The key factor of this particular tackle is timing. Misjudging your 'lunge' can lead to an unscheduled trip head first into the solid oak advertising hoarding, via the highly abrasive cinder track. It should be noted that the application of iodine upon a lacerated buttock is an indignity the Association is well advised to
ISSUED BY
BRINGING THE BALL DOWN
THE OVER
COFFMORE CIGARETTES
COFFMORE CIGARETTES
MORE CIGARETTES
SPORTSMANSHIP

UNLEASH THE POWER OF PUERILITY

GAME

THE GENTLEMAN'S GUIDE TO ASSOCIATION FOOTBALL

1

## How to kick the ball.

One of the commonest faults seen in Association Football is that of kicking the ball with the 'instep' whereas it should be kicked with the toe of the boot. To ensure executing this correctly; keep your head down, eyes on the ball, weight on your supporting foot, and swing the leg with all possible might in order to exert full power to the toe. However, it is all too easy to overlook one vital factor. Making contact with the ball. Lashing at fresh air can cause great indignity for the Association Footballer not to mention unnecessary strain on his athletic truss.

ISSUED BY

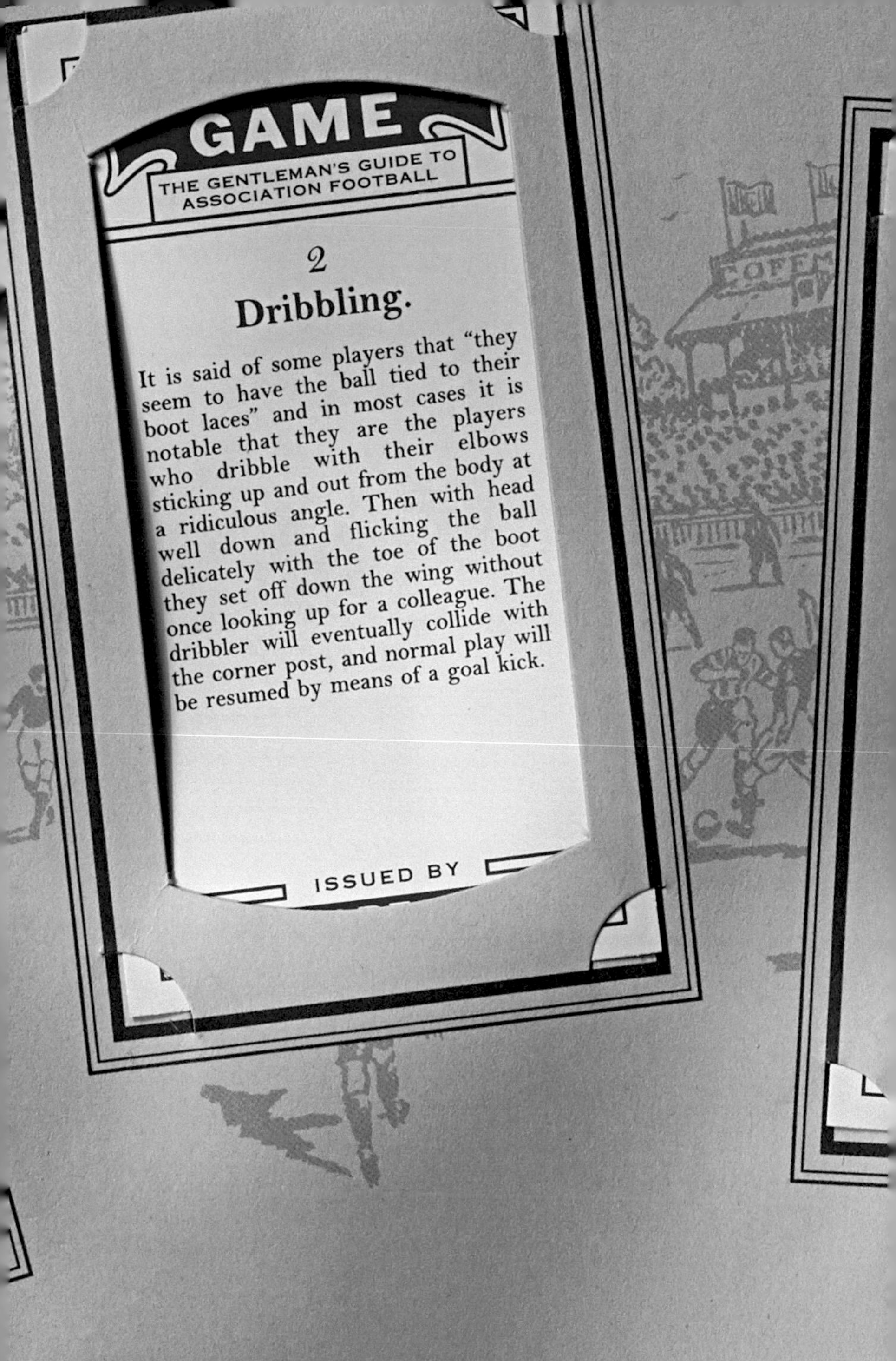
GAME

THE GENTLEMAN'S GUIDE TO ASSOCIATION FOOTBALL

2

**Dribbling.**

It is said of some players that "they seem to have the ball tied to their boot laces" and in most cases it is notable that they are the players who dribble with their elbows sticking up and out from the body at a ridiculous angle. Then with head well down and flicking the ball delicately with the toe of the boot they set off down the wing without once looking up for a colleague. The dribbler will eventually collide with the corner post, and normal play will be resumed by means of a goal kick.

ISSUED BY

NOW A STAR
OF THE
NATIONAL
FOOTBALL
MUSEUM

flicker
paff
nut
piff-piff
twat
shuffle
crunnch
rat-a-tat

*boot*

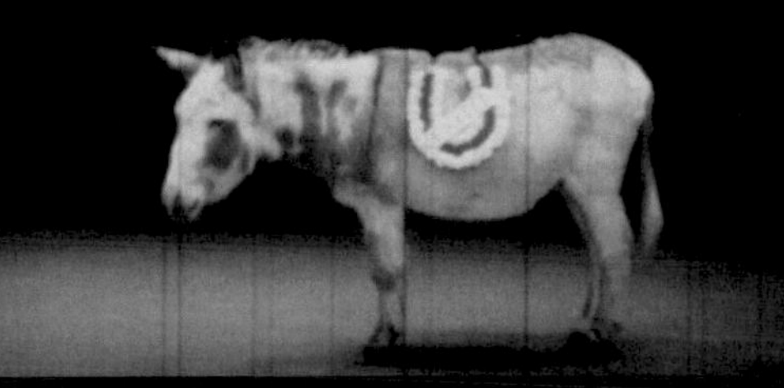

*bray*

*piff*

*sproing*

*twirl*

*tip-tip-tip*

*hurrah!*

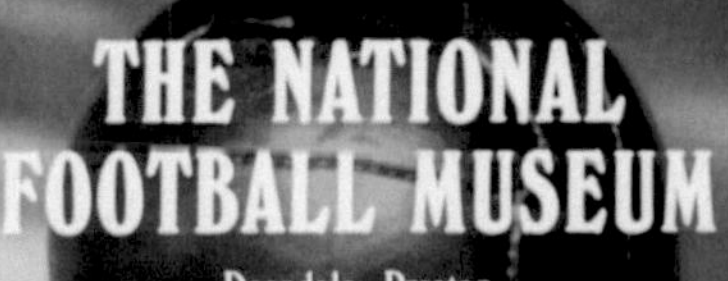


*spin*

*"and once again it's Bottomshuffle at the corner...*

*...My, what a splendid corner!"*

TUF-SHEET
Luxury non-absorbent
LAVATORY PAPER

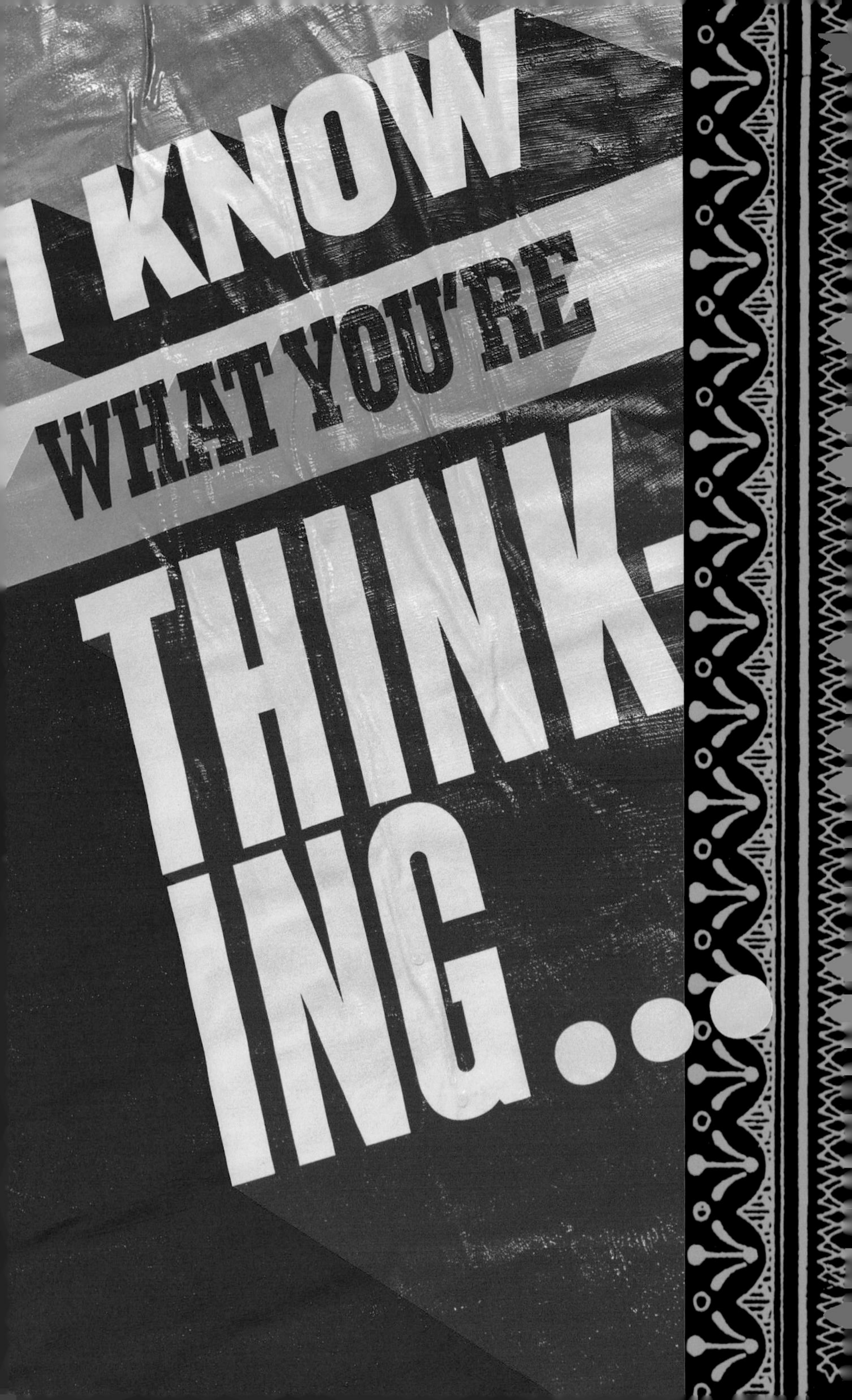
I KNOW
WHAT YOU'RE
THINK-
ING...

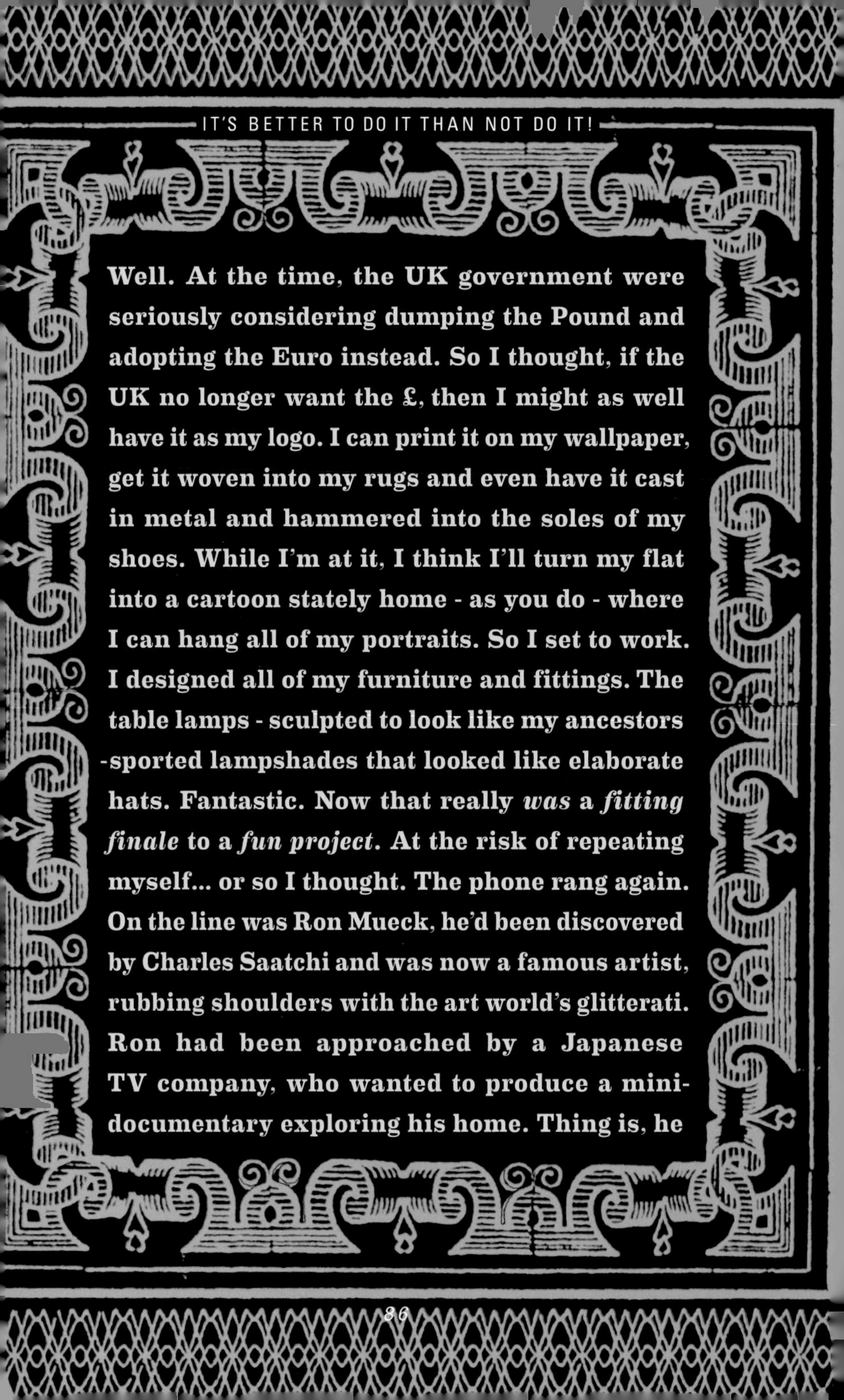

Well. At the time, the UK government were seriously considering dumping the Pound and adopting the Euro instead. So I thought, if the UK no longer want the £, then I might as well have it as my logo. I can print it on my wallpaper, get it woven into my rugs and even have it cast in metal and hammered into the soles of my shoes. While I'm at it, I think I'll turn my flat into a cartoon stately home - as you do - where I can hang all of my portraits. So I set to work. I designed all of my furniture and fittings. The table lamps - sculpted to look like my ancestors - sported lampshades that looked like elaborate hats. Fantastic. Now that really *was* a *fitting finale* to a *fun project*. At the risk of repeating myself... or so I thought. The phone rang again. On the line was Ron Mueck, he'd been discovered by Charles Saatchi and was now a famous artist, rubbing shoulders with the art world's glitterati. Ron had been approached by a Japanese TV company, who wanted to produce a mini-documentary exploring his home. Thing is, he was worried that they'd be a bit disappointed with his perfectly nice, but normal, semi in Tufnell Park. He figured what they really needed was a ridiculous cartoon stately home - did I want a half hour programme on Japanese TV all about my flat? My response: "Where do I sign?" On the day of the shoot, the producer had fun going through my wardrobes and pulling out my custom-made clothes. They were every bit as flamboyant as the colourful trappings around the flat. The only problem was, she was going to interview me in Japanese. Which explains why, when the programme aired, I have a very confused expression on my face. I couldn't really understand the questions so I didn't know whether I'd answered them or was ordering a ham sandwich. It was a *spectacularly* fine finale to a fun project. And yes, that actually is the ending. As the crew were packing up and leaving, I paused for a moment and looked at Malcolm's original picture of Nobby and thought. "*Yep, it's definitely better to do it than not do it.*"

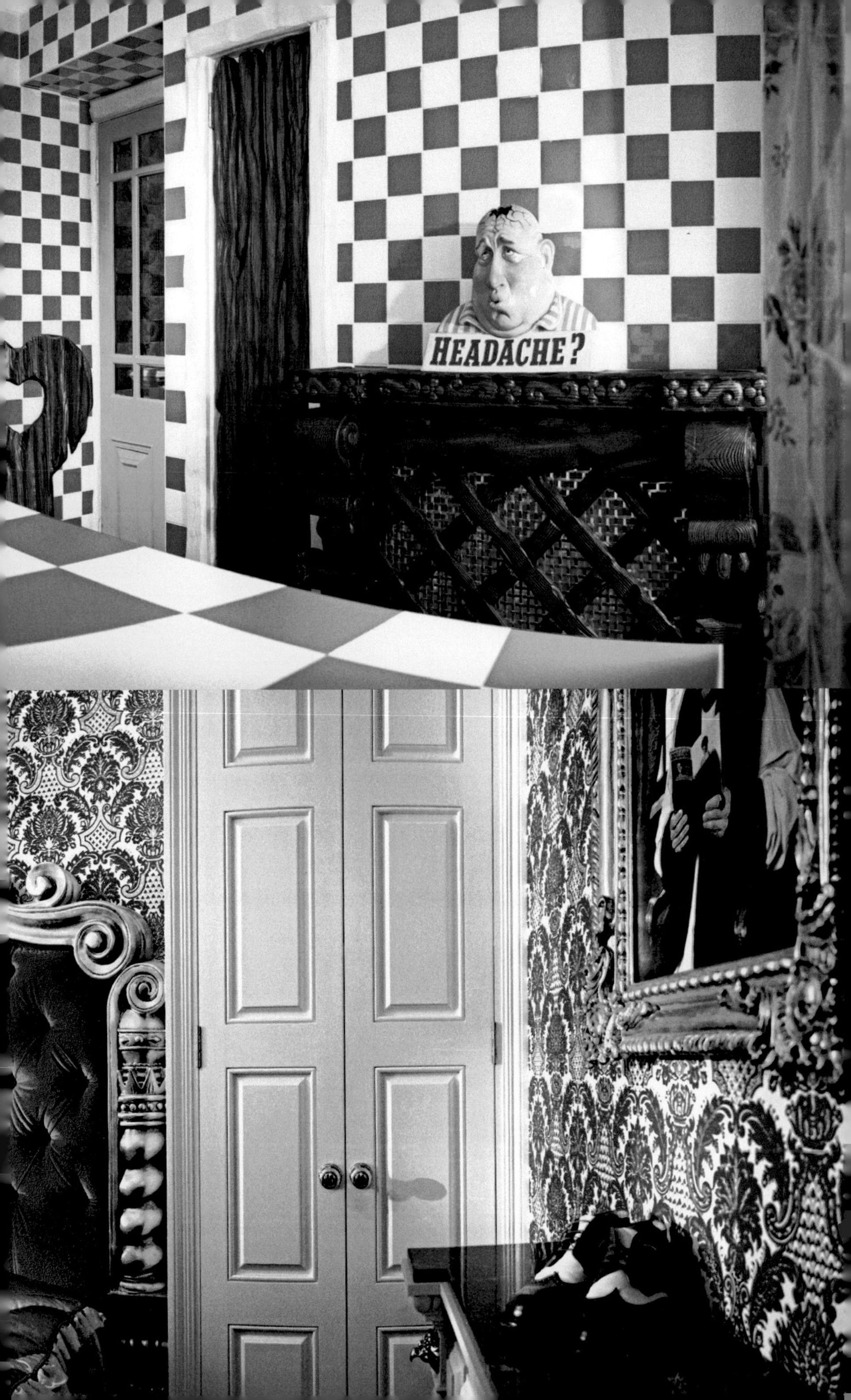
HEADACHE?

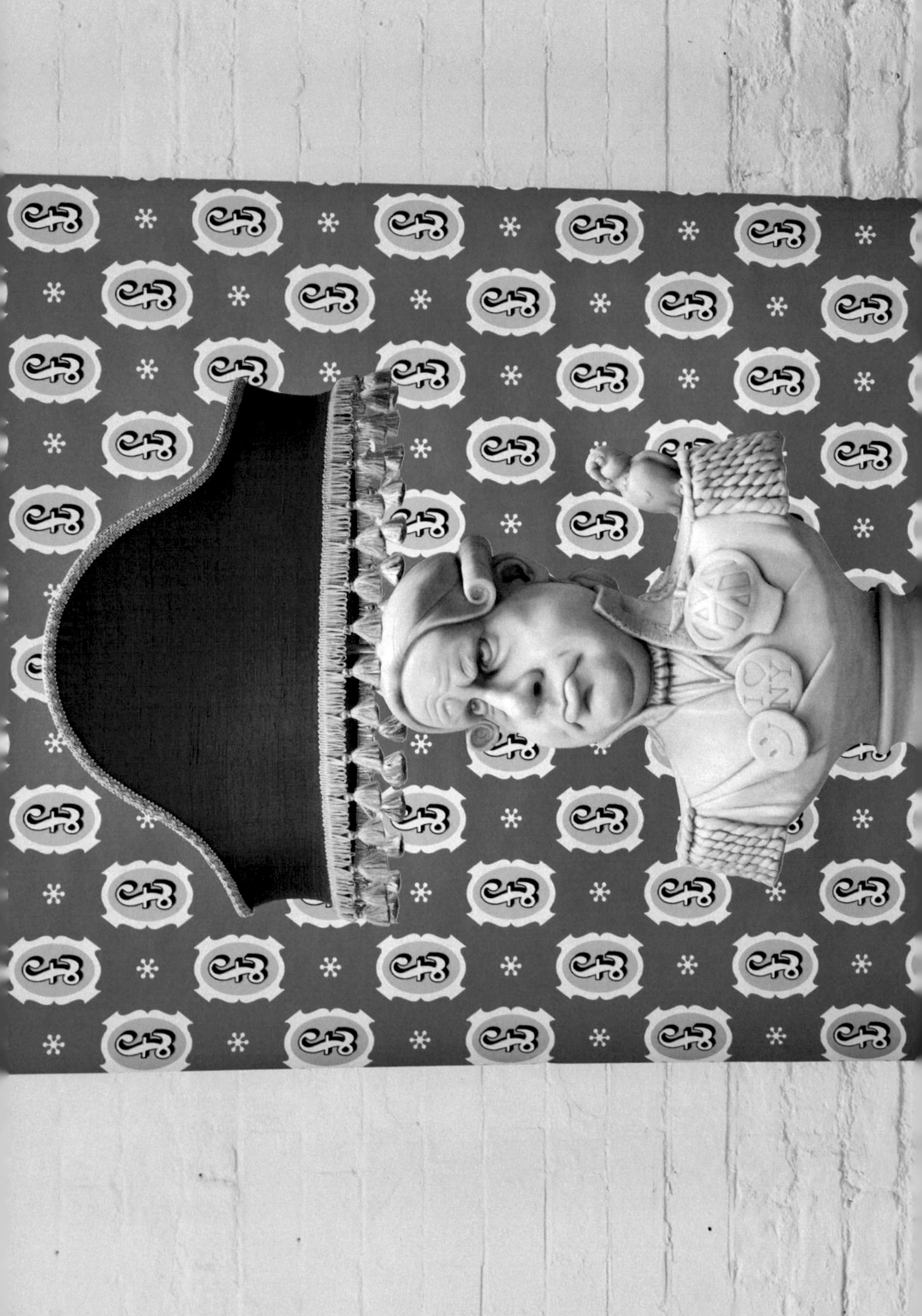

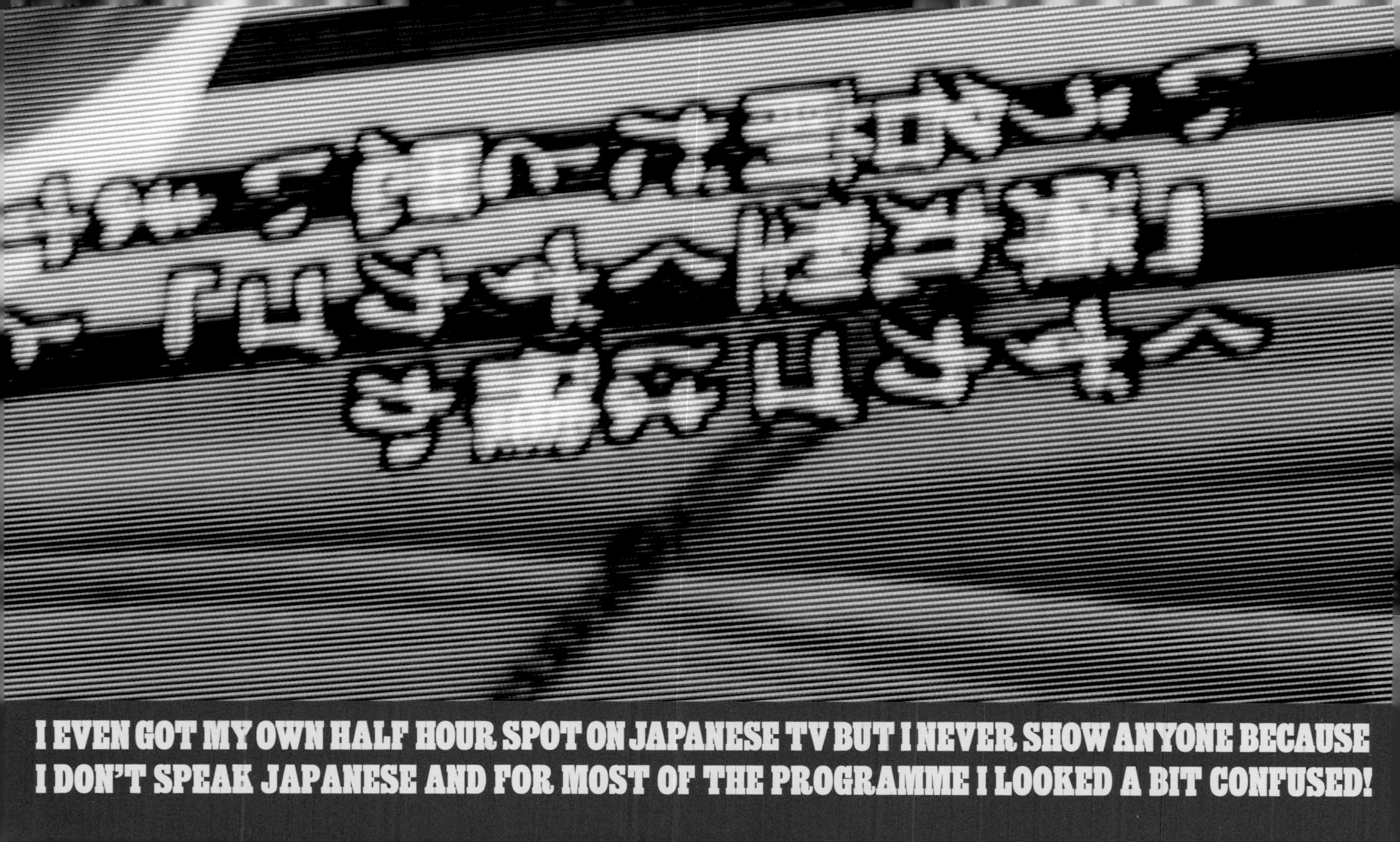

I EVEN GOT MY OWN HALF HOUR SPOT ON JAPANESE TV BUT I NEVER SHOW ANYONE BECAUSE I DON'T SPEAK JAPANESE AND FOR MOST OF THE PROGRAMME I LOOKED A BIT CONFUSED!

DON'T

TOO

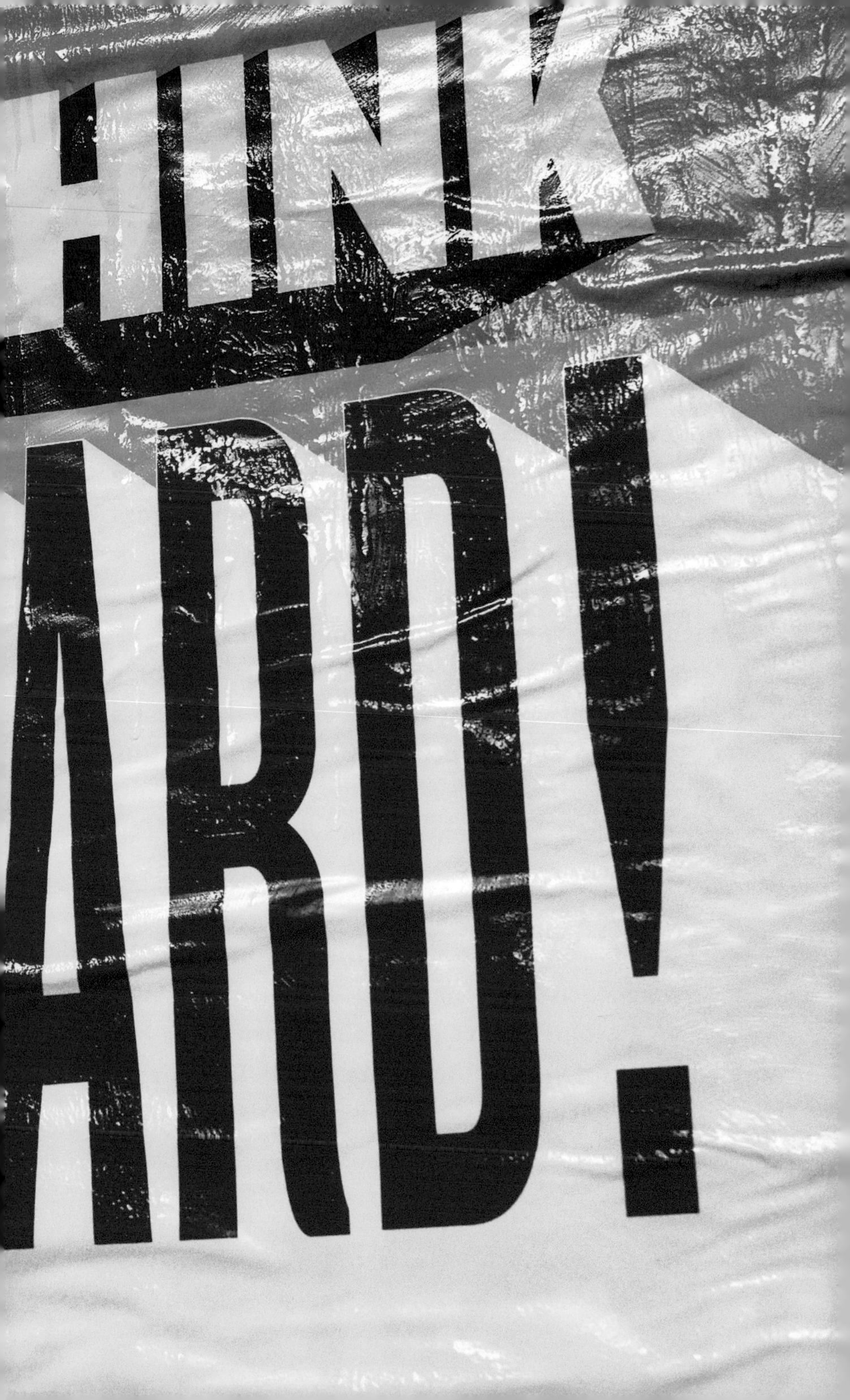
HINK
ARD!

**My day job is directing TV Commercials, and a few years ago I was working out of Blink - arguably London's hottest production company. Blink was originally set up by James Studholme, a terrific producer and a truly creative individual. Blink's London offices reflected this. Works of art were everywhere; and the walls, floors and furnishings were an eclectic amalgamation of design and decor, each component carefully considered. James himself was - still is - quite a dandy with his shock of ginger curls and bold check suits. Image is important to him, evident in everything he does, so when James decided that Blink's identity needed an overhaul, he hired a super-trendy designer to do it. Trouble was, when the work was delivered he wasn't too keen, so he asked me to overhaul the overhaul. I admit, my first response was to say no. I'd done this sort of thing for production companies before and, unsurprisingly given their line of work, they'd proved to be... shall we say... difficult and demanding clients. Or - to put it bluntly - a total nightmare. But James**

BLINK

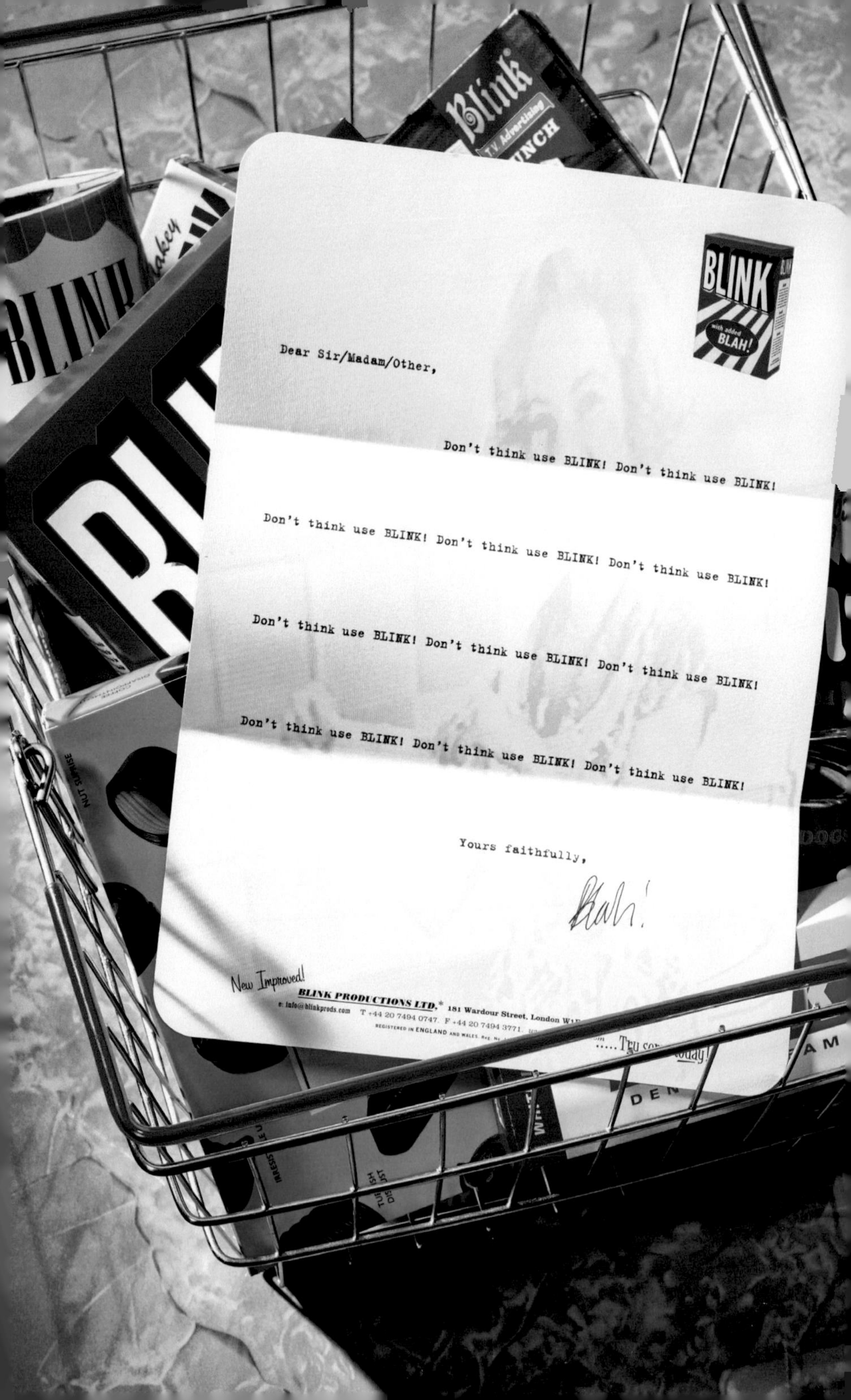

Dear Sir/Madam/Other,

Don't think use BLINK! Don't think use BLINK!

Don't think use BLINK! Don't think use BLINK! Don't think use BLINK!

Don't think use BLINK! Don't think use BLINK! Don't think use BLINK!

Don't think use BLINK! Don't think use BLINK! Don't think use BLINK!

Yours faithfully,

Blah!

BLINK
DENTAL CREAM
HOUSEHOLD
BLINK
1/-
WORKS COMPLETELY ROUND THE BEND
SOAPY
Blink
FOR HANDS THAT DO DITCHES
15 fl oz
BLINK
TUFF SHEET
Luxury Toilet Tissue
1/-
HARD BUT FAIR
Chocky
blink
6D
Blink
Blink
NEW!
Blink
WITH EXTRA COMPLIMENTS
BLINK
with added BLAH!

**twisted my arm and eventually I caved in, "On one condition: you have to give me a completely free hand." To my amazement, he agreed. So I happily rolled up my sleeves and got stuck in. I came up with two very different ideas. The first was based on images of an owl with huge, staring eyes, being tortured in various ways, accompanied by a speech bubble shouting "BLINK!" from an unseen torturer. The second idea was based on what Blink actually did: make TV commercials. For this, I recalled the ads I'd loved when I was growing up. Wouldn't it be good, I thought, if every time you saw the word *Blink*, it was the brand name on something like a packet of soap powder, a choccy bar or a bottle of fizzy pop? All the images would be just like those from that classic era of TV advertising, complemented by a slogan that could also have come from the same period: 'Don't think. Use *Blink*.' James loved it, and '*Blinky*' the tortured owl was never mentioned again. So the fun began. I scoured junk shops for old packaging, bottles and cans and set about**

Husky!
BLINK
NEW!
Blink
WITH EXTRA COMPLIMENTS
So tempting!
BLINK PRODUCTIONS LTD, 181 Wardour Street, London W1F 8WZ.
★ Tel +44 20 7494 0747. Fax +44 20 7494 3771 ✻ e:info@blinkprods.com www.blinkprods.com
.....m-m-m-m!

designing a full range of 'Blink' products. The main image was a packet of soap powder, which bore a smiling 1950s housewife proudly presenting a pair of whiter-than-white pants. Back then, directors' showreels were sent out on U-Matic tapes; big, bulky grey lumps. Every agency TV department had shelves groaning with U-Matics and they all looked exactly the same, except for the small logos within the tiny plastic sleeves on their identical grey boxes. I decided to encase the Blink showreel in a bright red cardboard sleeve, which was designed to look like a box of Blink soap powder, *'Now with added BLAH!'* They sang out amongst the sea of grey like ridiculously radiant red things. And that set the tone for everything. Blink's identity became big, brash and bold. Which translated as confident, creative and colourful. James was paying for all this, so the budget wasn't limitless. I pulled my usual stunt of corralling family and friends to dress up as the characters I needed. The starring role of '1950s Soap Powder Housewife' went to Elizabeth

**Trustram (Truzz), a production manager who worked at Blink. While '1960s Girl Promoting Blink Corned Beef' was my lovely stepdaughter, Saskia Laroque Rothstein-Longaretti. Truzz even appeared on the Blink letterhead, which had a rosewood-effect envelope, inspired by those vintage TV cabinets from the fifties. Inside the envelope was a TV screen containing an image from a Blink toothpaste ad, which revealed itself once the letter was removed. Soon I didn't have to think too hard, I saw potential Blink products wherever I looked: Blink Toilet Tissue -'No.1 for No.2s', Blink Carpet Cleaner-'9/10 Mats Prefer It', Blink Washing-Up Liquid-'For Hands That Do Ditches'. The cornier the better because Blink's stunning body of film work was anything but. A while later, when U-Matics were being replaced by DVDs, a DVD-sized Blink cover was needed. So I designed one that looked like a packet of budgie food, emblazoned with the slogan '*Makes Your Budgie Pounce With Stealth*', based on the old Trill budgie food line, '*Makes Your Budgie Bounce With Health*'.**

**Once the Blink logo had been tastefully deposited on the back in budgie poo - the effect was complete. The Blink brand identity went on to win graphic design awards all over the world, including the Grand Award for Design at New York Festivals. James was delighted and came back with another little project. He wanted a compilation DVD to showcase the work of all Blink's directors. My response was immediate and instinctive, "You don't want a compilation DVD, what you really want is a comedy box of chocolates." I'd always trusted my instincts, but luckily, James now trusted them too. He kindly left me alone to concoct the custom-made chocs. They had names like, 'Fudge Dread', 'Turkish Disgust', 'Salt 'n' Vinegar' and (my personal favourite) 'Coffee Disappointment - not everyone's cup of tea.' The Blink identity was one of my all-time favourite jobs and James was the perfect client, true to his word when it came to giving me a free hand. As I recall, he only ever turned down one *Blink* product: 'Chocolate Starfish'. I can't for the life of me imagine why.**

For hands

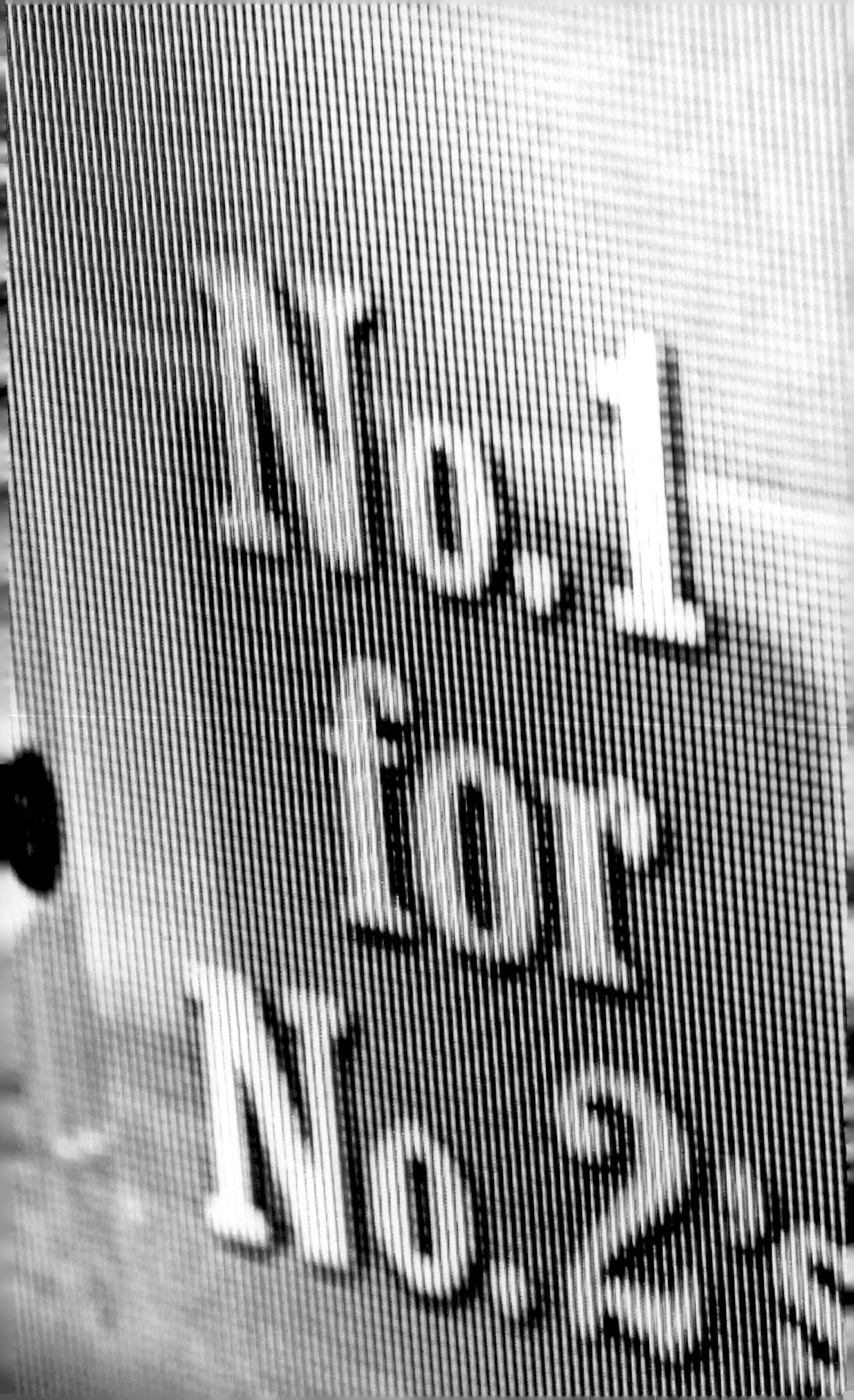
No 1
for

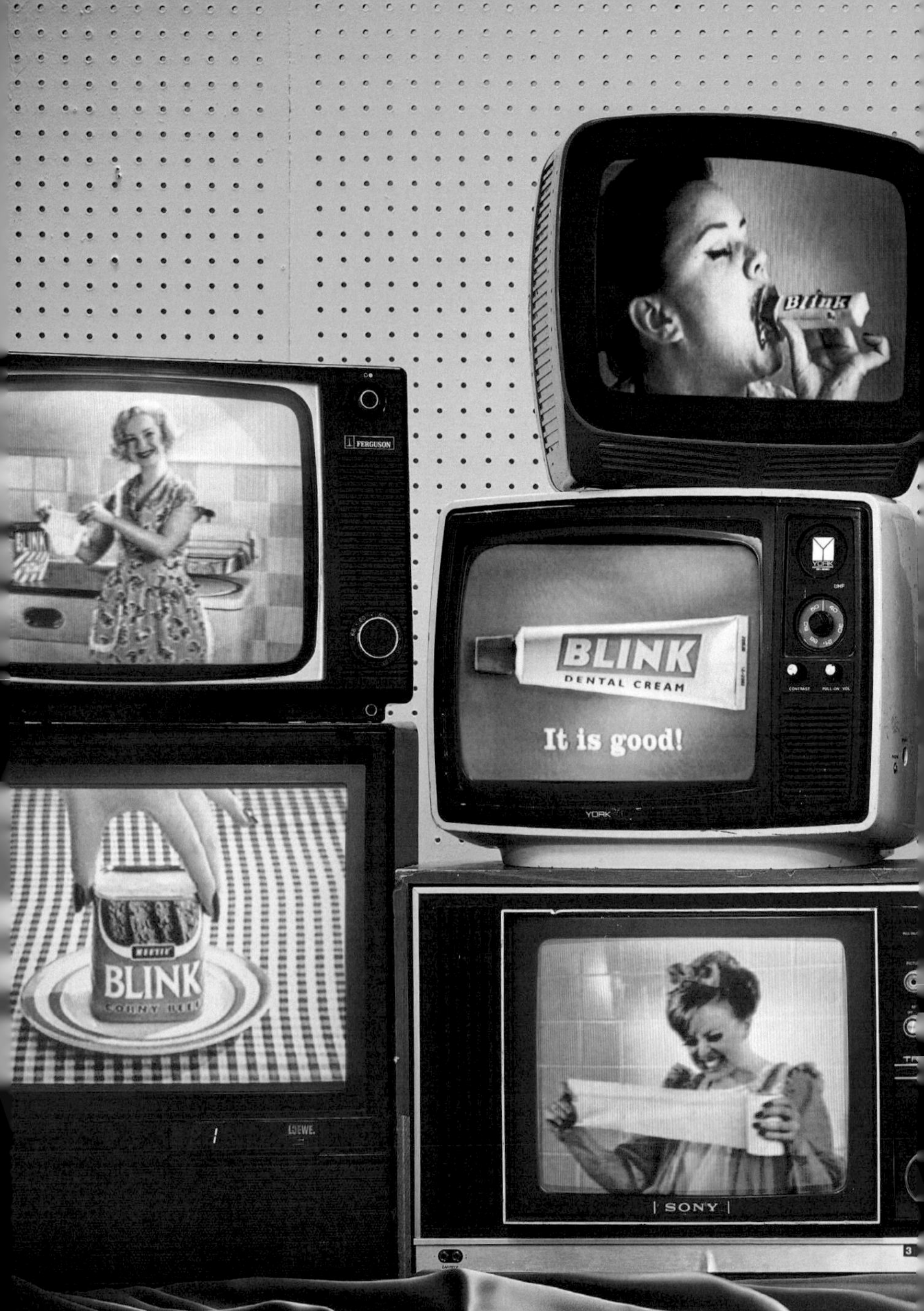
Blink
FERGUSON
BLINK
DENTAL CREAM
It is good!
YORK
BLINK
LOEWE.
SONY

BLINK
carpet cleaner
9 out of 10 mats prefer it!
BLINK
BLINK
For hands that do ditch
"THEY'RE...
R-R-R-RUFF!"
Blink

2/6
CHEEP
Blink
BUDGIE FOOD
Makes your Budgies POUNCE with Stealth!
1lb NET WT

FUDGE DREAD

IRRESISTIBLE URGE
NUT SUPRISE
SALT 'N' VINEGAR
TURKISH
DISGUST
Blink
SELECTION
FUDGE DREAD
NAUGHTY BOY
RUM DOO
CRÉME
SYNTHETIQUE
NUT SUPRISE
HEART de BERNE
E2257 TRUFFLE

**NAUGHTY BOY**
A Devilishly
Delinquent Deposit

**RUM DOO**
Nautical but Nice

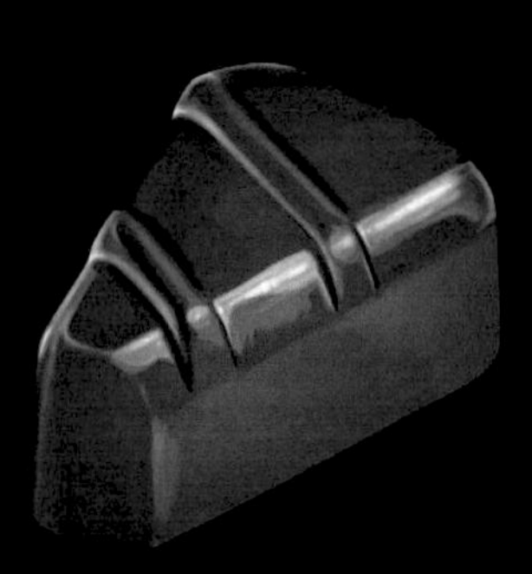

**COFFEE DISAPPOINTMENT**
Not everyone's
cup of Tea

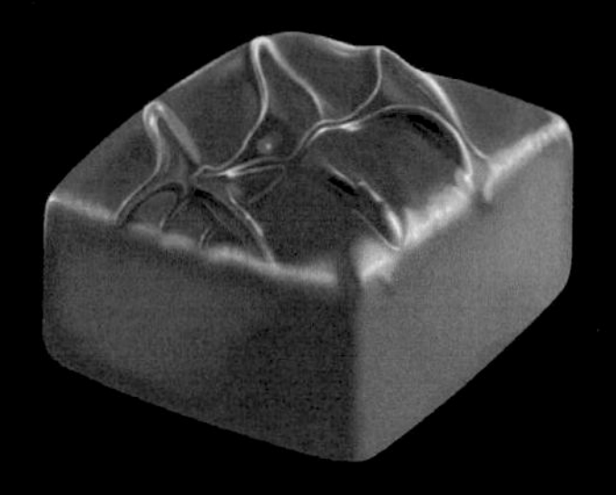

**FUDGE DREAD**
Dreamy Fudge
astride a runny
Chocolate Bottom

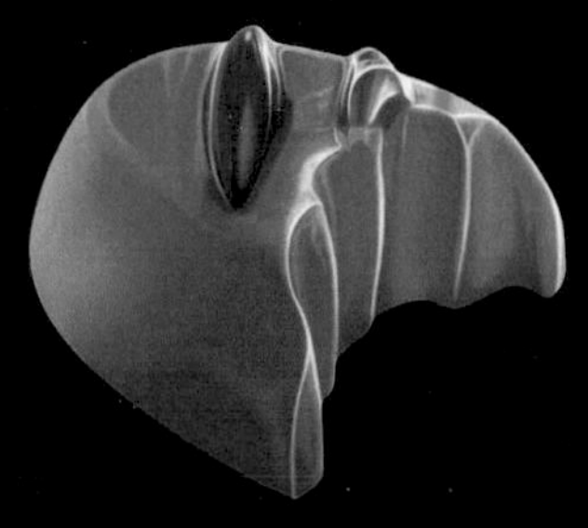

**IRRESISTIBLE URGE**
Bitter Dark Chocolate
enrobed in Bitten Milk
Chocolate

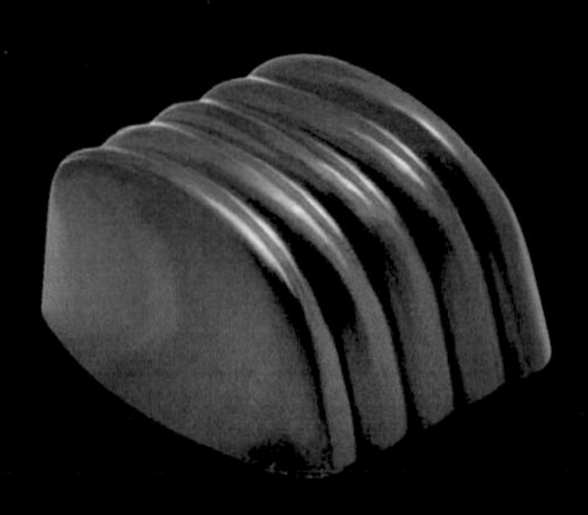

**TURKISH DISGUST**
Like Turkish Delight
only without the Delight

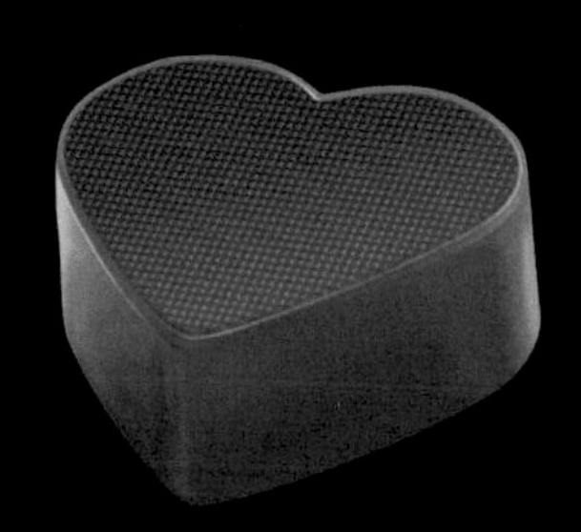

HEART de BERNE
A Haunting Experience
that will visit you
Again and Again

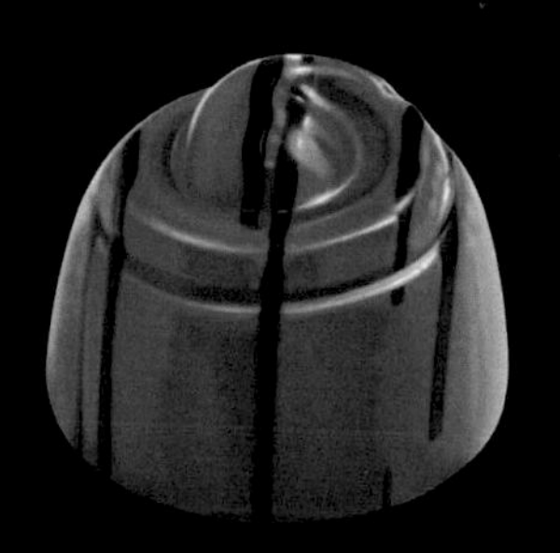

CRÉME
SYNTHETIQUE
Fruits of the Laboratory
smothered in Chocolate

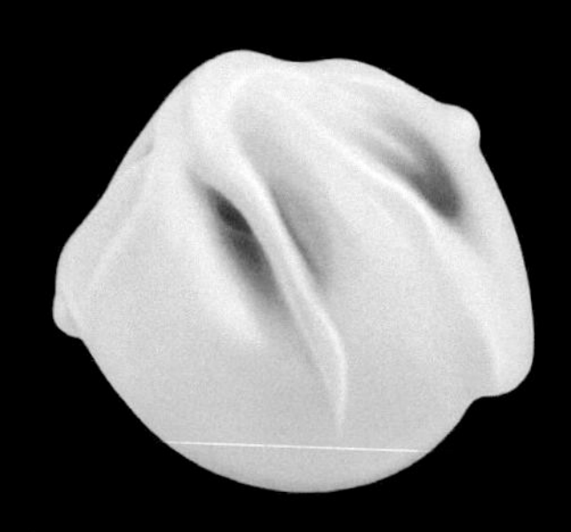

E2257 TRUFFLE
Zesty E2557 seductively
cloaked in E58913

SALT 'N' VINEGAR
Seductive Chocolate
with a distinctive
crisp flavour

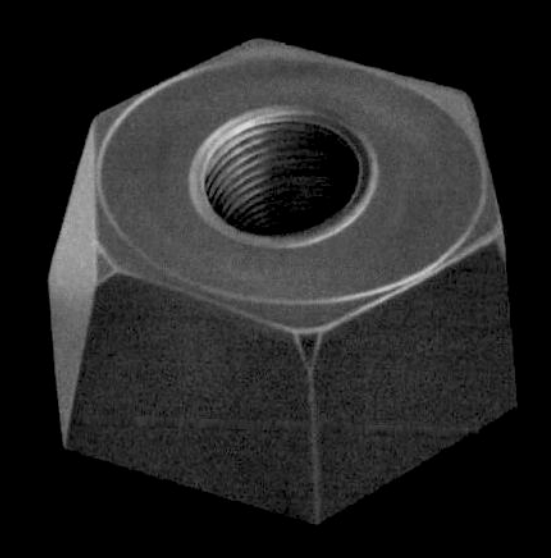

NUT SURPRISE
A Bolt of Inspiration
encased in Chocolate

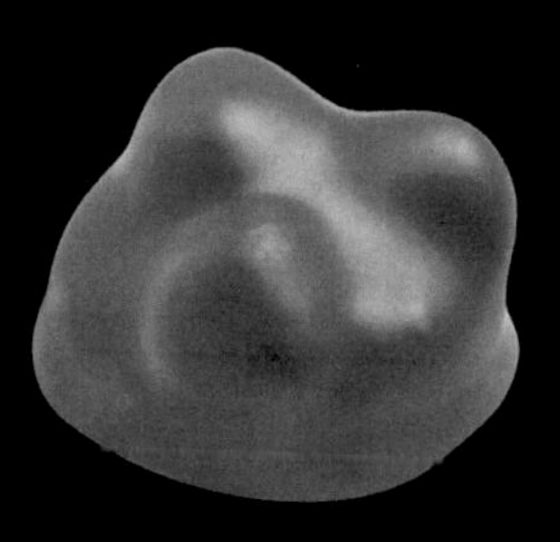

BOMBE CLUSTER
A Taste Explosion
awaiting your Disposal

**'GINGER JIM' based on the boss of Bli**

oductions, Sir Lord James Studholme Esquire.

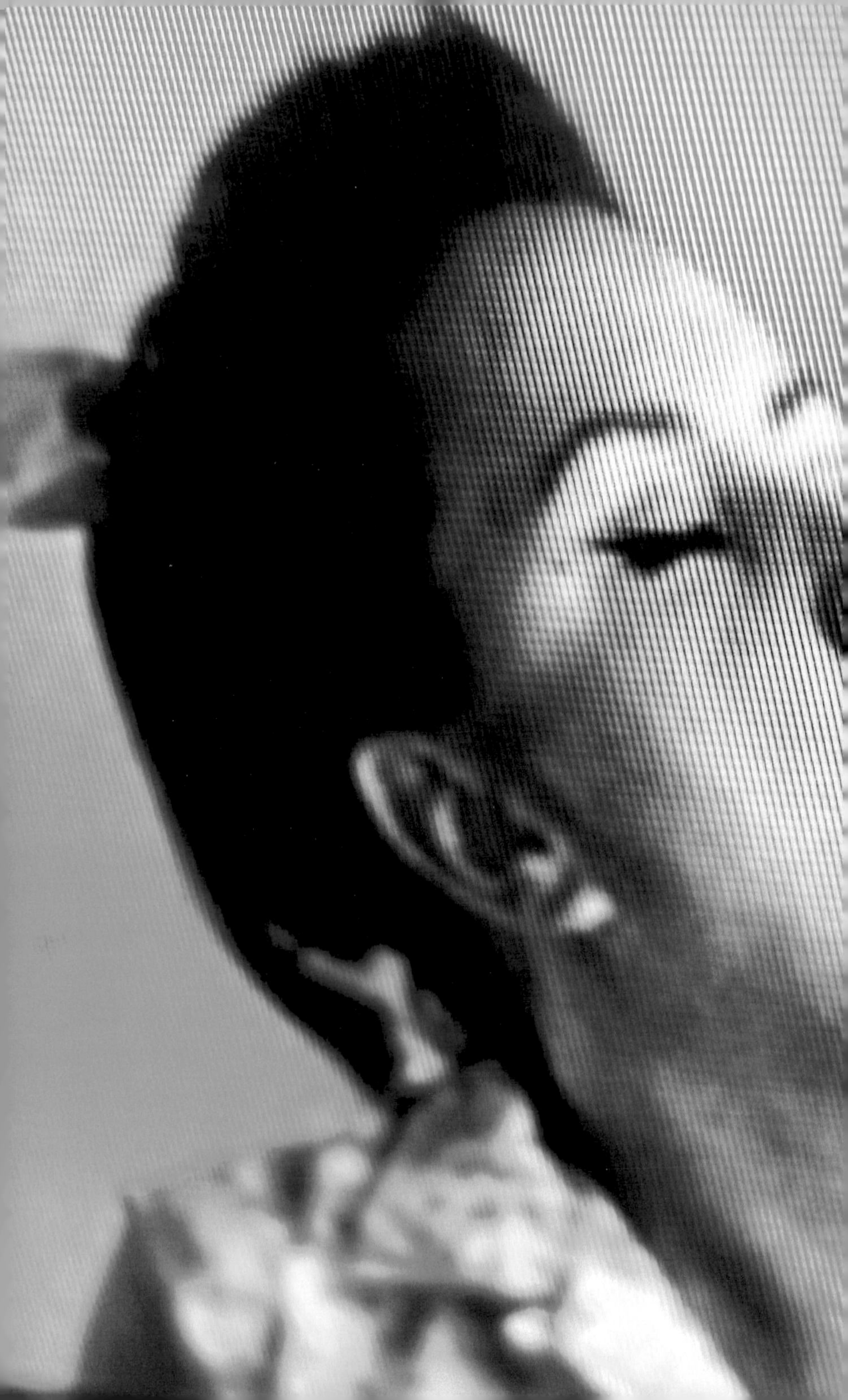

THE BE

of a

MA

DEBA

**Oh, come on. You knew what you were getting into. The title of the book must have been a bit of a clue. After a decade of directing, I thought it was time I introduced myself to the new generation of creatives who were too young to remember me in my heyday. I cast my mind back to what had always inspired me when I was a fledgling art director. And I could sum it up in one word: awards. Big, shiny gongs. I couldn't wait to win a few because, I thought, a shelf groaning with trophies would prove to the world (but more importantly, to me) that I'd been blessed with some kind of talent. So then, to appeal to the youngsters, I decided to create a magazine all about advertising awards and design it in the style of the publications I used to find in the woods as a kid. Back then, before such imagery moved online, you could seldom walk more than a hundred yards in the local woods before stumbling across a stack of nudie books: adult magazines with titles like '*Parade*' or '*Health & Efficiency*'. I began**

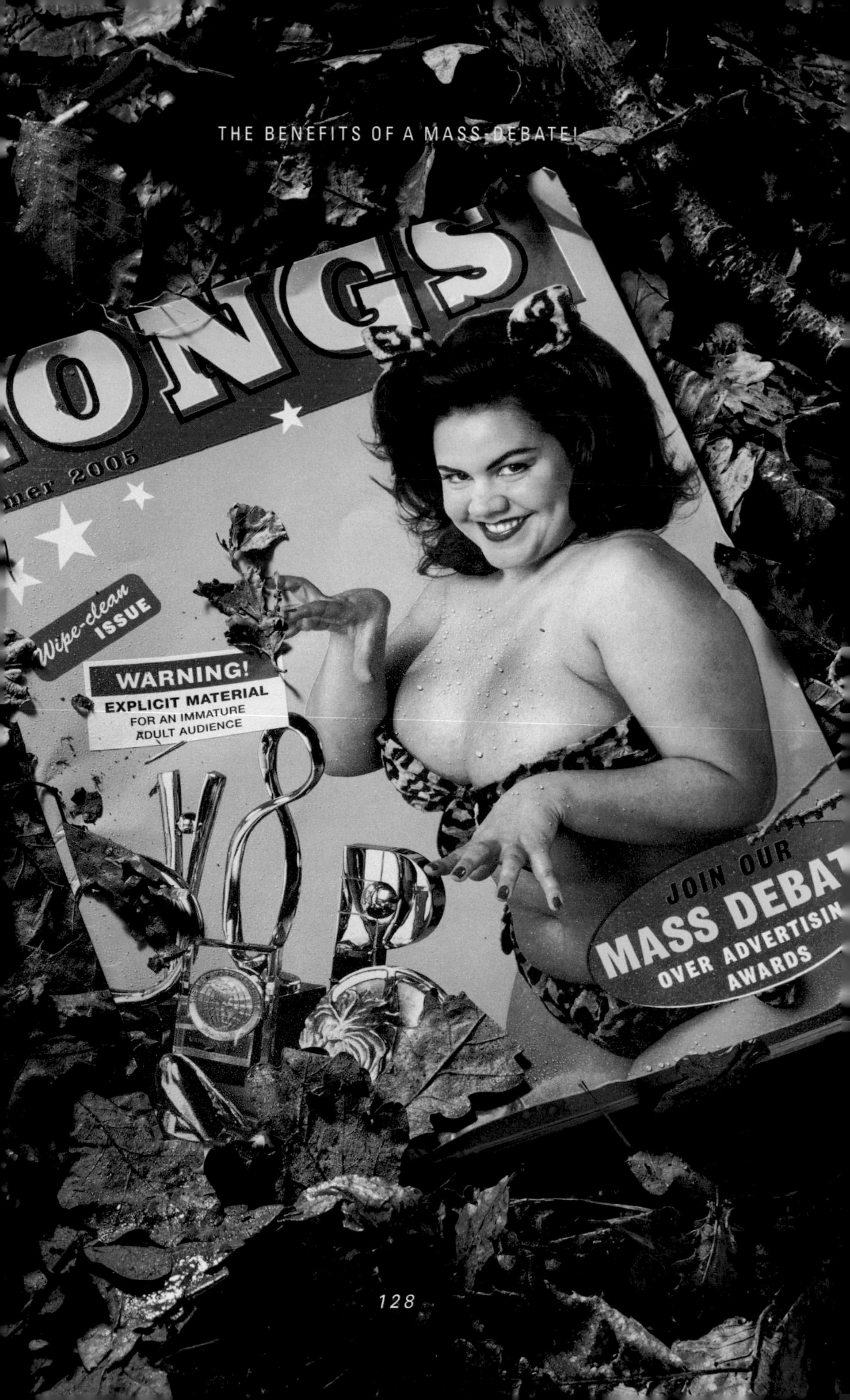

ONGS
mer 2005
Wipe-clean ISSUE
WARNING!
EXPLICIT MATERIAL
FOR AN IMMATURE ADULT AUDIENCE
JOIN OUR
MASS DEBAT
OVER ADVERTISIN
AWARDS

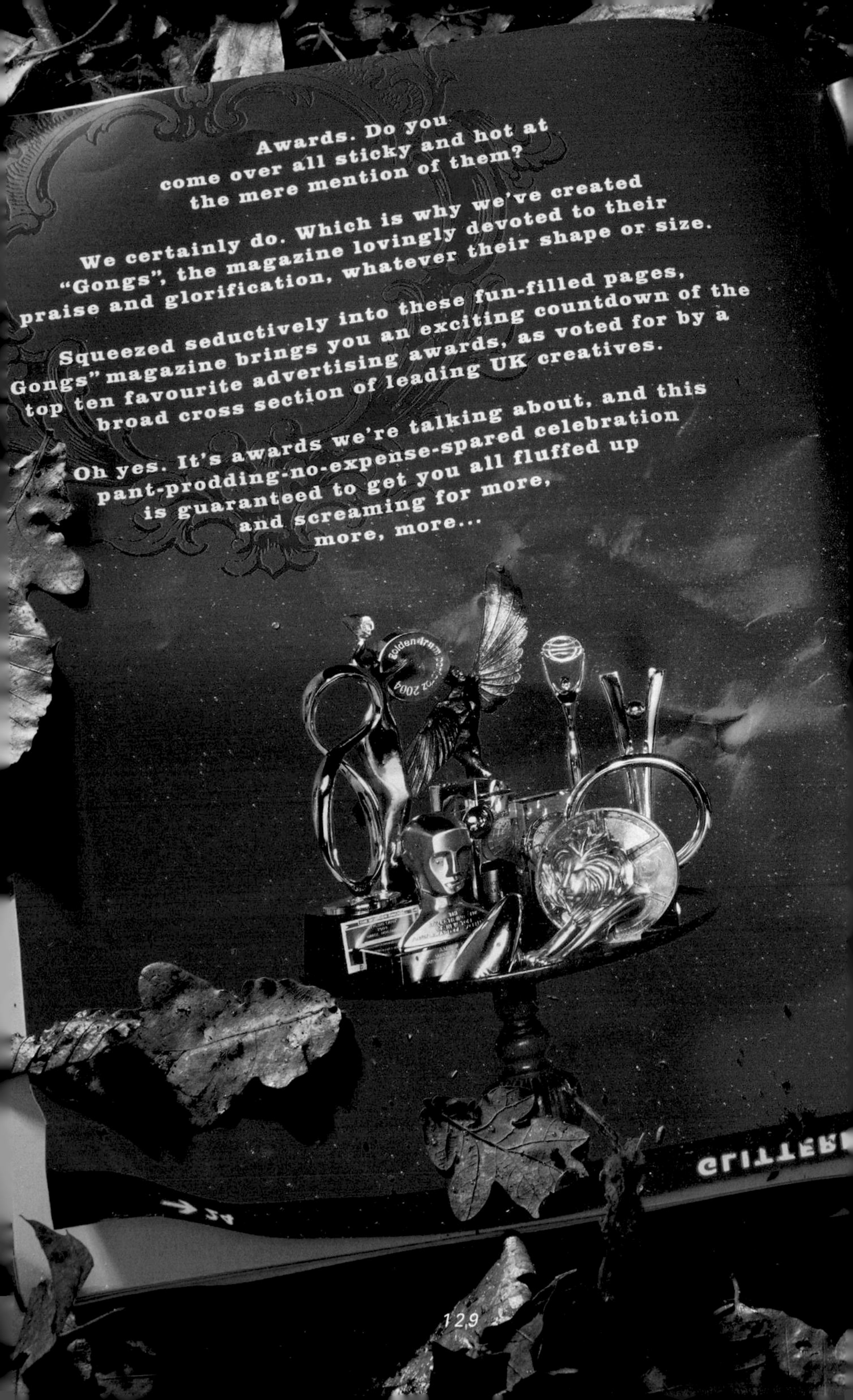

Awards. Do you
come over all sticky and hot at
the mere mention of them?

We certainly do. Which is why we've created
"Gongs", the magazine lovingly devoted to their
praise and glorification, whatever their shape or size.

Squeezed seductively into these fun-filled pages,
"Gongs" magazine brings you an exciting countdown of the
top ten favourite advertising awards, as voted for by a
broad cross section of leading UK creatives.

Oh yes. It's awards we're talking about, and this
pant-prodding-no-expense-spared celebration
is guaranteed to get you all fluffed up
and screaming for more,
more, more...

by doing some research in the form of direct mail asking creatives what their favourite advertising awards were. They sent me their answers on a postcard. I took their top ten and allotted points for Golds, Silvers, Bronzes and Certificates. I was then able to compile the Top 50 most awarded Art Directors and Copywriters over the previous ten years. The advertising industry has always been fuelled by ego, so I thought I'd stir things up a bit by publishing my findings. One of the postcards came back with a handwritten note scrawled on its bottom, "Have you thought about running any advertising in your magazine?" Well, no I hadn't. The suggestion had come from the smart and inventive Ed Morris - then a star creative at Lowe Howard-Spink - and it was a belter. This was only meant to be a promotional piece but I took up Ed's suggestion and set about selling advertising space in the publication. With one proviso - I didn't want just any ads in it. No, this would be the first magazine to only accept *good* advertising. And of course, London's creative community would be only too happy to provide it. A few weeks later I watched it roll off the press; a magazine called '*GONGS*', all about advertising awards. It was designed like a vintage nudie mag and filled with great press ads, many of which went on to win awards in their own right. Now before anyone gets too sensitive about the concept, it wasn't salacious. In fact, it was almost innocent, and, as an early advocate of diversity, I made *sure* there was something in it for everyone. Naturally, there had to be a knees-up and the launch party at 'Sketch' in London was one of the most spectacular I've ever hosted. Images from the magazine were projected all around this huge space; there was drinking, dancing and free tubs of Styling Lard, specially made for the occasion. Did it get me any extra work? Probably. But I couldn't say for certain. Only one thing I can say for certain: It was a flippin' good night.

vaceous cutie for your delectation and delight.
go to any wavelengths to tune into this bashful beauty.

TEN

SEV
Feast your eyes
on a pictorial
celebration of
the fuller figure.
Rounded, curvy
and with a big
sexy bottom.

Didn't anyone tell you it's rude to stare? One look at this baby and it won't be long before Cupid's own little arrow makes an appearance.
35

WHEN IT
COMES TO SHOWING OFF A
TRULY STUNNING PAIR, THESE
TWO BEAUTIES ARE THE **D&ADY**

★

**2B OR NOT 2B?** WHO CARES
AS LONG AS THEY'RE BLACK
OR YELLOW

# THE HOTTEST ONE [H]UNDRED!

NOW you've drooled over our bevy of **BEAUTIES**, here are some of the lucky recipients who've had their grubby mitts on them.

- It's our very own list of the UK's **top 50** Art Directors and Copywriters over the last 10 years.
- Extensive research was conducted, which, amongst other things, included: spinning a **bottle,** rolling **dice** and sticking a **pin** into a long list of candidates.
- We eventually concluded that the fairest method of calculation was to create a league table, based on **points** accrued from D&AD, Campaign Press, Campaign Posters & BTAA. (D&AD being worth more points because it topped our straw poll).
- We only included **golds and silvers,** no effectiveness, overseas or design categories.
- Bronze and commendations were also **left out** because, frankly, by that stage we had the complete arse ache with it.
- **Apologies** for any glaring omissions we may have made. But to all those who made the list **congratulations** on your imminent pay rise.
- And to those that didn't, why not compile your own? After all you might have **plenty** of time on your hands soon.

**D&AD**

| | |
|---|---|
| Gold | 10 points |
| Silver | 8 points |
| Silver Nominations | 5 points |

**Campaign Press & Poster and [...]**

Gold

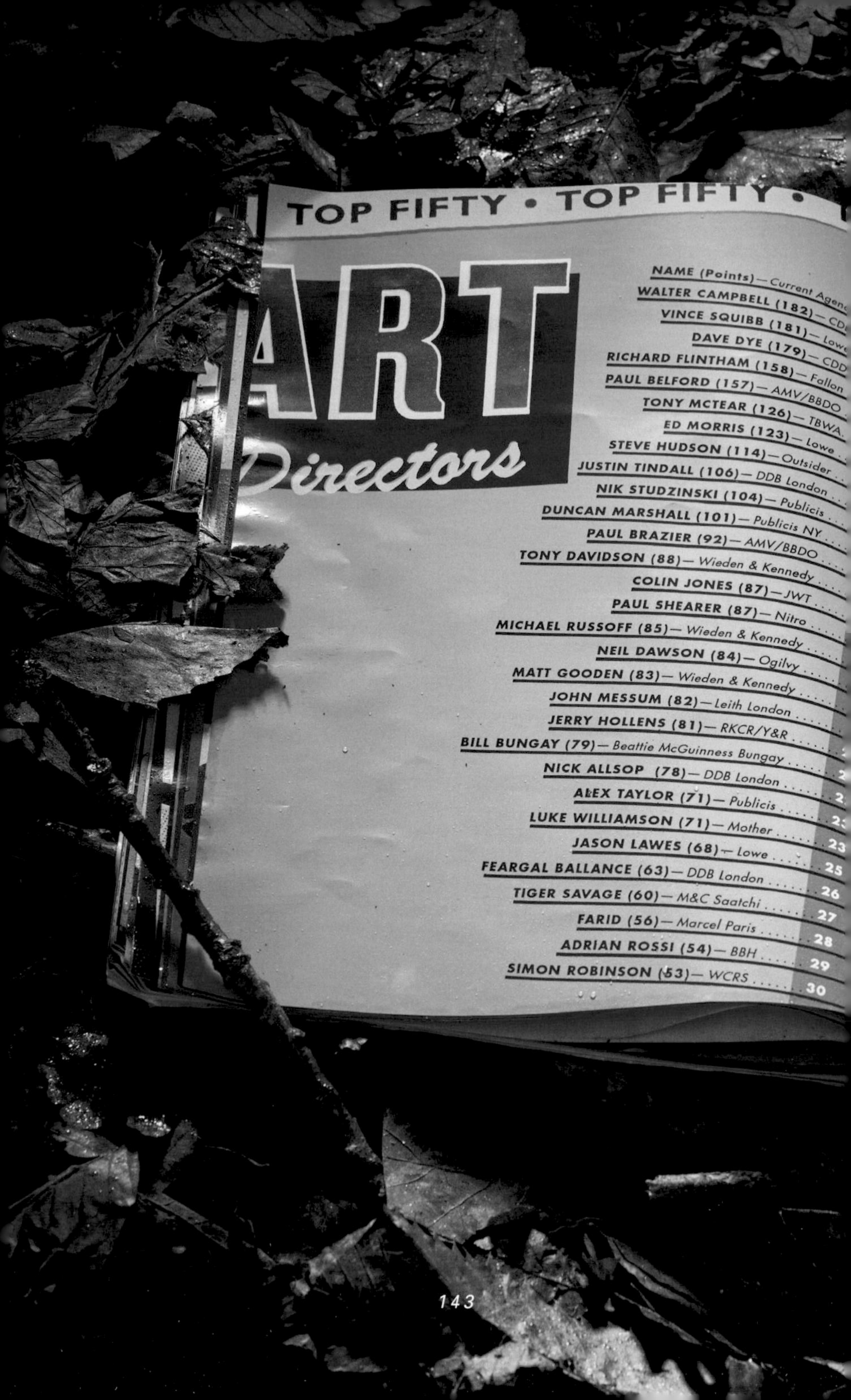

TOP FIFTY • TOP FIFTY •

# ART Directors

NAME (Points)—Current Agenc
WALTER CAMPBELL (182)—CD
VINCE SQUIBB (181)—Lowe
DAVE DYE (179)—CDD
RICHARD FLINTHAM (158)—Fallon
PAUL BELFORD (157)—AMV/BBDO
TONY MCTEAR (126)—TBWA
ED MORRIS (123)—Lowe
STEVE HUDSON (114)—Outsider
JUSTIN TINDALL (106)—DDB London
NIK STUDZINSKI (104)—Publicis
DUNCAN MARSHALL (101)—Publicis NY
PAUL BRAZIER (92)—AMV/BBDO
TONY DAVIDSON (88)—Wieden & Kennedy
COLIN JONES (87)—JWT
PAUL SHEARER (87)—Nitro
MICHAEL RUSSOFF (85)—Wieden & Kennedy
NEIL DAWSON (84)—Ogilvy
MATT GOODEN (83)—Wieden & Kennedy
JOHN MESSUM (82)—Leith London
JERRY HOLLENS (81)—RKCR/Y&R
BILL BUNGAY (79)—Beattie McGuinness Bungay
NICK ALLSOP (78)—DDB London
ALEX TAYLOR (71)—Publicis
LUKE WILLIAMSON (71)—Mother
JASON LAWES (68)—Lowe . . . . . 23
FEARGAL BALLANCE (63)—DDB London . . . . . 25
TIGER SAVAGE (60)—M&C Saatchi . . . . . 26
FARID (56)—Marcel Paris . . . . . 27
ADRIAN ROSSI (54)—BBH . . . . . 28
SIMON ROBINSON (53)—WCRS . . . . . 29
. . . . . 30

ANDY SMART (52) — CDP-Travissully ...... 31
MARK TUTSELL (49) — Leo Burnett, Chicago ...... 32
IAN DUCKER (49) — Vinnie ...... 32
JOHN GORSE (46) — ? ...... 34
DAMON COLLINS (45) — Mother ...... 35
ROSIE ARNOLD (45) — BBH ...... 35
BRIAN CAMPBELL (41) — TBWA ...... 37
JOANNA WENLEY (41) — DDB London ...... 37
PAUL ANGUS (41) — RKCR/Y&R ...... 37
MIKE DURBAN (38) — AMV/BBDO ...... 40
ANDY AMADEO (38) — Mustoes ...... 40
DAVE MASTERMAN (36) — BBH ...... 42
GRANT PARKER (36) — DDB London ...... 42
ADAM CHIAPPE (35) — MCBD ...... 44
GUY MOORE (35) — Leo Burnett ...... 44
GRAHAM STOREY (32) — AMV/BBDO ...... 46
STUART OUTHWAITE (32) — Mother ...... 46
KEITH COURTNEY (32) — Publicis ...... 46
GRAEME NORWAYS (31) — Freelance ...... 49
GLEN GIBBINS (30) — Fallon ...... 50

59

...I wanted to make sure the

***as something in it for everyone!***

# Images from the magazine we

rojected all around this huge space...

***...There were drinks, dancin***

*ad free tubs of Styling Lard.*

Styling
LARD™
EXTRA FIRM HOLD

YOU
THER

PY!

**No, not you personally. And not that kind of therapy. This was just a slogan I'd written for Therapy Films, another production company producing TV commercials. But 'Therapy' wasn't just any production company; it belonged to my old friend Malcolm Venville, who'd made a very successful transition from photographer to director. Of course he had. Malcolm had such a good eye that it was only a matter of time before he started shooting moving images as beautifully as he'd always shot stills. Anyway, he called me to ask if I'd like to join Therapy as his business partner. I was flattered, delighted, and immediately keen to give Therapy a brand new identity; whether they wanted one or not. Fortunately, Malcolm is always open to novel ideas. My train of thought for the new Therapy brand identity went like this: Therapy. Psychiatry. Napoleon's hat. That's it. Anyone who's ever seen a person wearing a Napoleon hat in a cartoon, or in a 1970s sketch show (unless that person is supposed to be Napoleon) knows it's shorthand**

# THERAPY

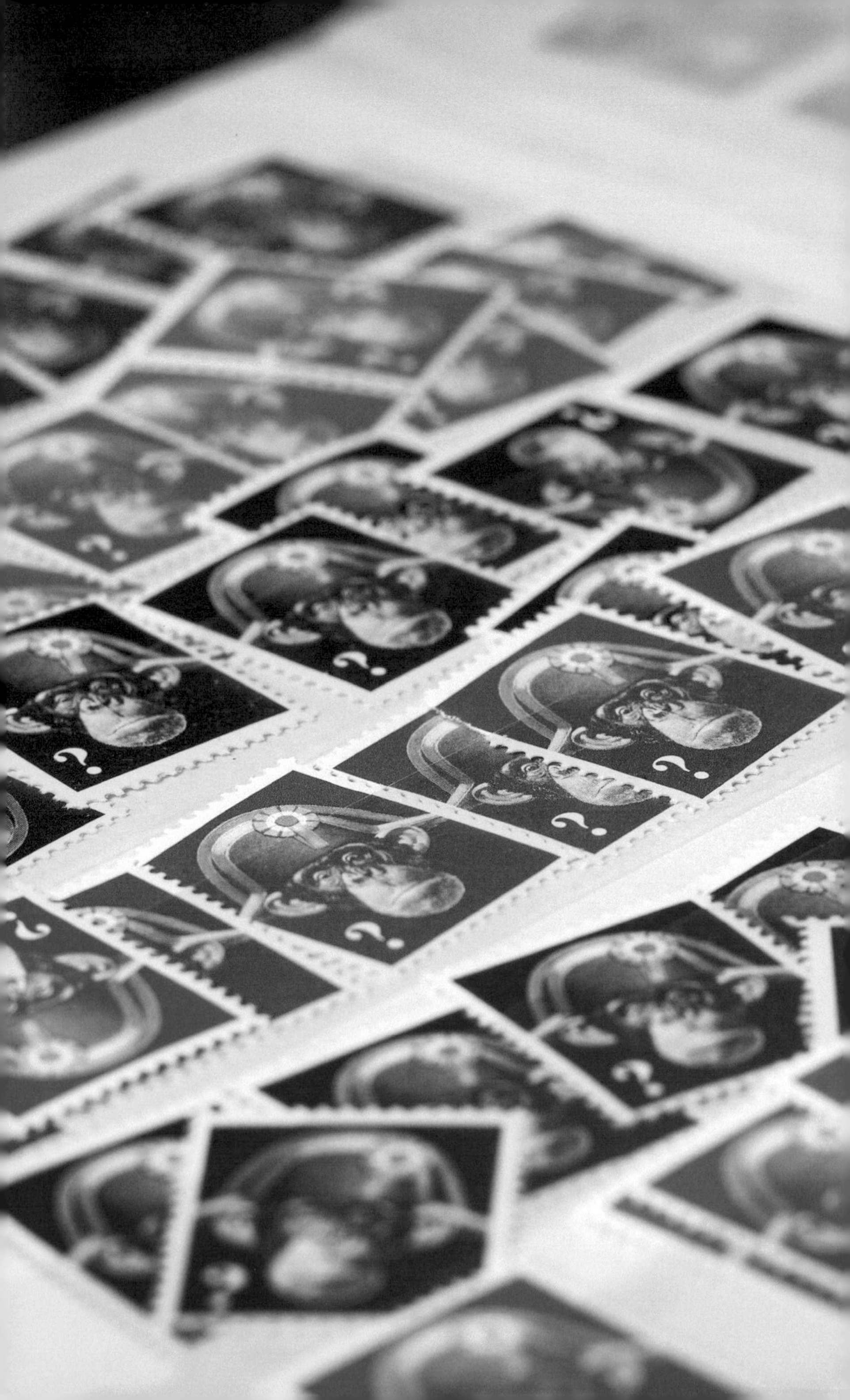

for some kind of delusional disorder. So why put a Napoleon hat on a monkey? The answer is, because I really, really, really, like monkeys. Ergo, the new Therapy logo: a monkey in a Napoleon hat. The letterhead would be bound up like a straitjacket and all the business cards would feature images alluding to madness; a cuckoo clock, a potty, a fruitcake, some crackers... you get the idea. Showreels were sent out in a custom-made bag, which had a load of nuts printed on the inside and came with a free banana embellished with a blue Napoleon monkey sticker. It was such fun to work on that I kept adding extra items to the range. Like a collection of Therapy stamps, and a Therapy telegram. Yes, a telegram. In the age of email, don't you think there's something rather special about a telegram? Far less disposable and completely un-deletable... Or perhaps you think they're just pointlessly insane? Probably a bit of both. So if this all seems a bit special but insane to you, then I'm delighted. That means the Therapy identity was definitely 'on brand'.

THERAPY
YOU NEED THERAPY. YOU NEED THERAPY. YOU NEED THERAPY.
YOU NEED THERAPY. YOU NEED THERAPY. YOU NEED THERAPY.
YOU NEED THERAPY. YOU NEED THERAPY. YOU NEED THERAPY.
YOU NEED THERAPY. YOU NEED THERAPY. YOU NEED THERAPY.
YOU NEED THERAPY. YOU NEED THERAPY. YOU NEED THERAPY.
YOU NEED THERAPY. YOU NEED THERAPY. YOU NEED THERAPY.
YOU NE D THERAPY. YOUNNEED THERAPY. YOU NEED THERAPY.
YOU NEED THERAPY. YOU NEED THERAPY. YOU NEED THERAPY.
YOU NEED THERAPY. YOU NEED THERAPY. YOU NEED THERAPY.
YOU NEED THERAPY. YOU NEED THERAPY. YOU NEED THERAPY.
YOU NEED THERAPY. YOU NEED THERAPY. YOU NEED THERAPY.
YOU NEED THERAPY. YOU NEED THERAPY. YOU NEED THERAPY.
YOU NEED THERAPY. YOU NEED THERAPY. YOU NEED THERAPY.
YOU NEED THERABY. YOU NEED THERAPY. YOU NEED THERAPY.
YOU NEED THERAPY. YOU NEED THERAPY. YOU NEED THERAPY.
YOU NEED THERAPY. YOU NEED THERAPY. YOU NEED THERAPY.
YOU NEED THERAPY. YOU NEED THERAPY. YOU NEED THERAPY.
YOU NEED THERAPY. YOU NEED THERAPY. YPU NEED THERAPY
YOU NEED THERAPY. YOU NEED THERAPY. YOU NEED THERAPY
YOU NEED THERAPY. YOU NEED THERAPY. YOU NEED THERAP
YOU NEED THERAPY. YOU NEED THERAPY. YOU NEED THERAP
YOU NEED THERAPY. YOU NEED THERAPY. YOU NEED THERAP
THERAPY FILMS, 2ND FLOOR, 26 MARKET PLACE, LONDON W1W 8AN. TEL: 020
EMAIL: INFO@THERAPYFILMS.COM COMPANY NO. 4399385
REGISTERED OFFICE: 7-9 SWALLOW STREET, LONDON W1B 4DT

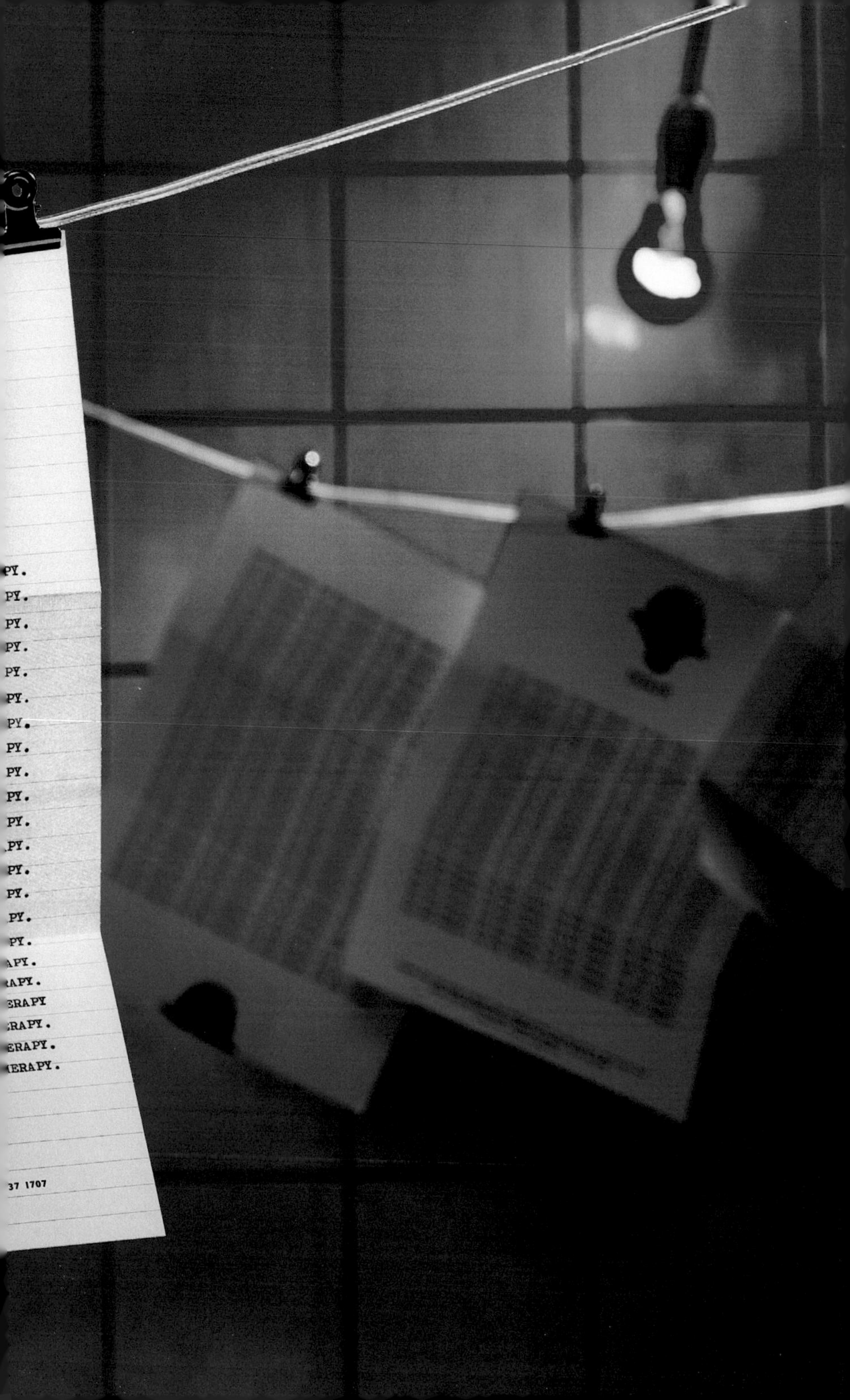

THERAPY
MALCOLM VENVILLE
020 7436 5191
MARK DENTON
020 7436 5191
MARK DENTON
020 7436 5191
MARK DENTON
020 7436 5191

GUY MANWARING
020 7436 5191
Y MANWARING
191
MALCOLM VENVILLE
020 7436 5191
THERAPY
MARK DENTON
SIMON LEVENE
020 7436 51

NEWS

YOU NEED THERAPY!
BLAH BLAH BLAH + STOP +
H BLAH BLAH BLAH BLAH + STOP +
H BLAH BLAH BLAH BLAH + STOP +
LAH BLAH BLAH + STOP +
H BLAH BLAH BLAH + STOP+
THERAPY NEWS
MAIL-O-GRAM
I SAID URGENT
SPECIAL RELEASE
TO WHOM IT MAY CONCERN.
FROM THERAPY
WOOF

Therapy
FOR EXTERNAL USE ONLY
Made in England
2ND FLOOR 26 MARKET PLACE
LONDON

YOU NEED
THERAPY
NEED THERAPY YOU NEED THERAPY YOU NEED THERAPY YOU
THERAPY

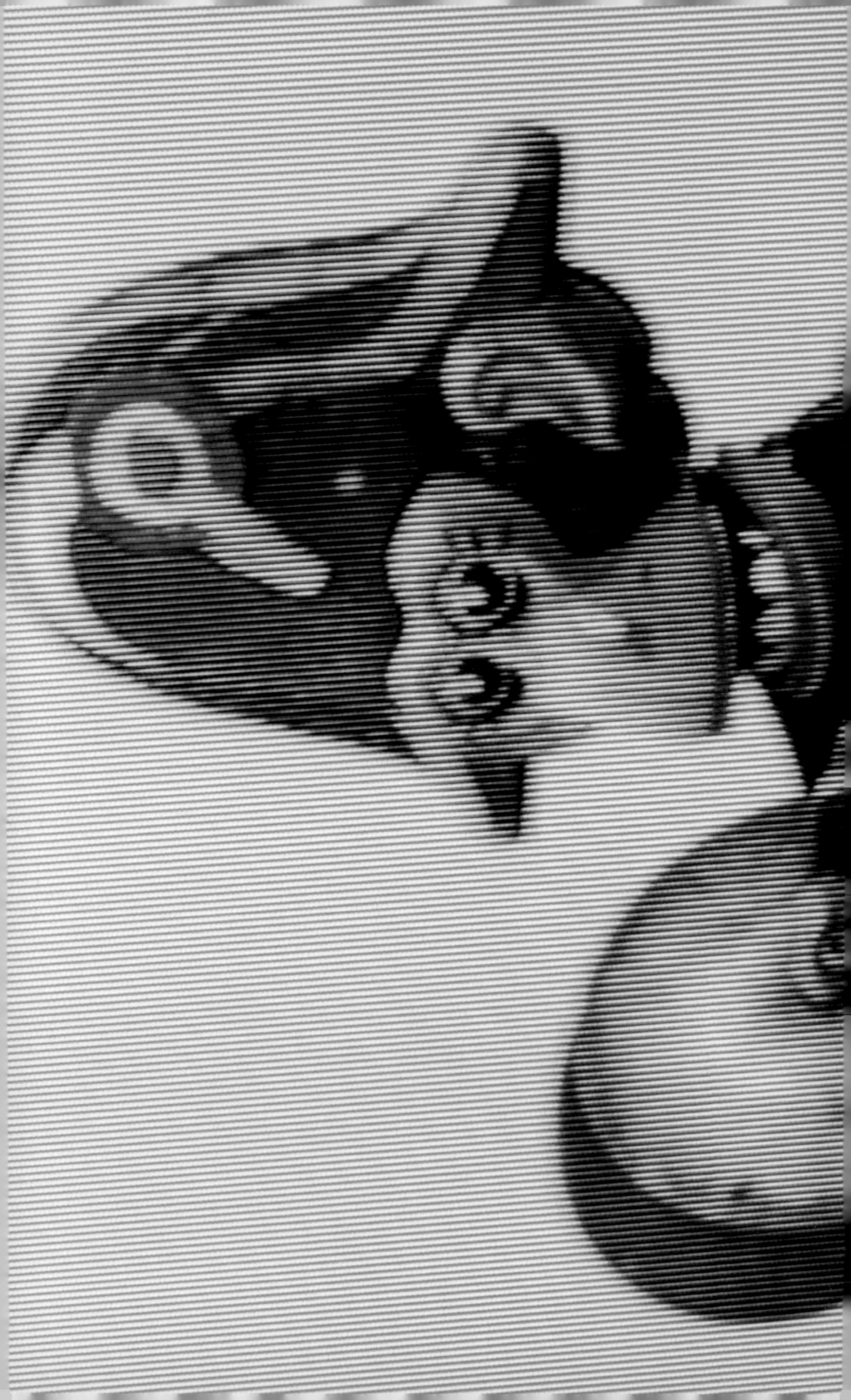

THERAPY

THERAPY

YOU NEED THERAPY
VIRAL
THERAPY

LONDON
Cuckoo! Cuckoo! Cuckoo! Cuckoo!

W YORK
L.A.
ckoo! Cuckoo! Cuckoo! Cuckoo! Cuckoo

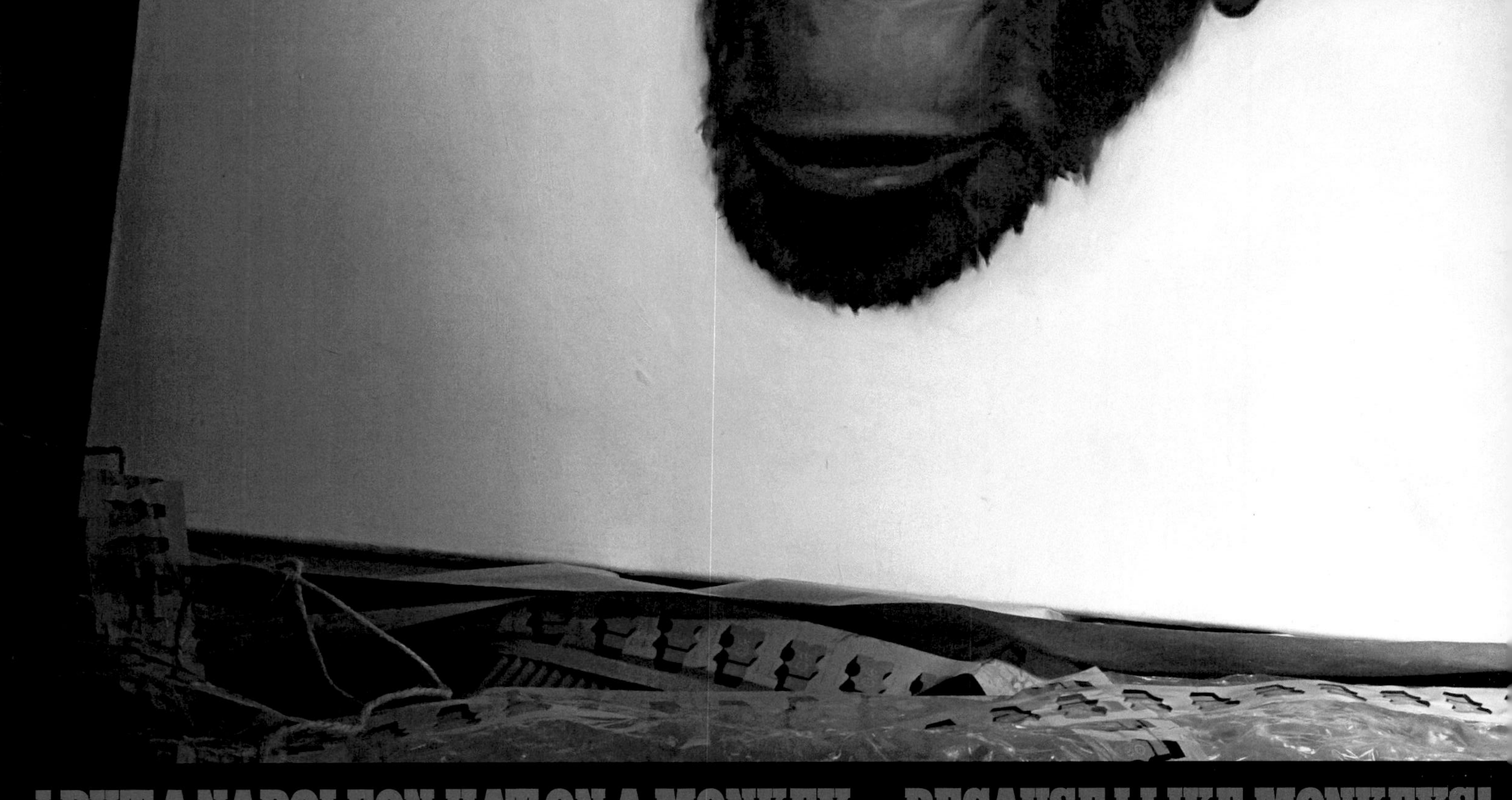

I PUT A NAPOLEON HAT ON A MONKEY... BECAUSE I LIKE MONKEYS!

PAYS

netimes

TO BE

VIL!

It started as a conversation between me and Guy Thomson, boss of the wonderful animation company (formerly) known as 'Moving House'. Guy was saying how he was happy with everything about that company (as well he might be). Everything, that is, except the name. I had to agree. It didn't reflect how good they were and actually, it was a bit misleading: it sounded like a firm of removal men. We decided that the name needed 're-moving'. So a meeting was set up and I dragged in some creative mates for a brainstorming session. We started shouting out suggestions: "Super-Winners!" "Lady Patricia Cakebread!" "A Large Evil Corporation!" Everyone laughed at the last one. It was suggested by a bright young spark called Rory McCaskill, and what made it especially funny was the fact that Guy's company was neither large nor evil. It was the very opposite: just Guy, his business partner (the brilliant animator Seth Watkins) and a small team. Once the laughter had died down, it was obvious that we'd found the perfect name. Guy hadn't requested a new identity but with a

EVIL
PLAN

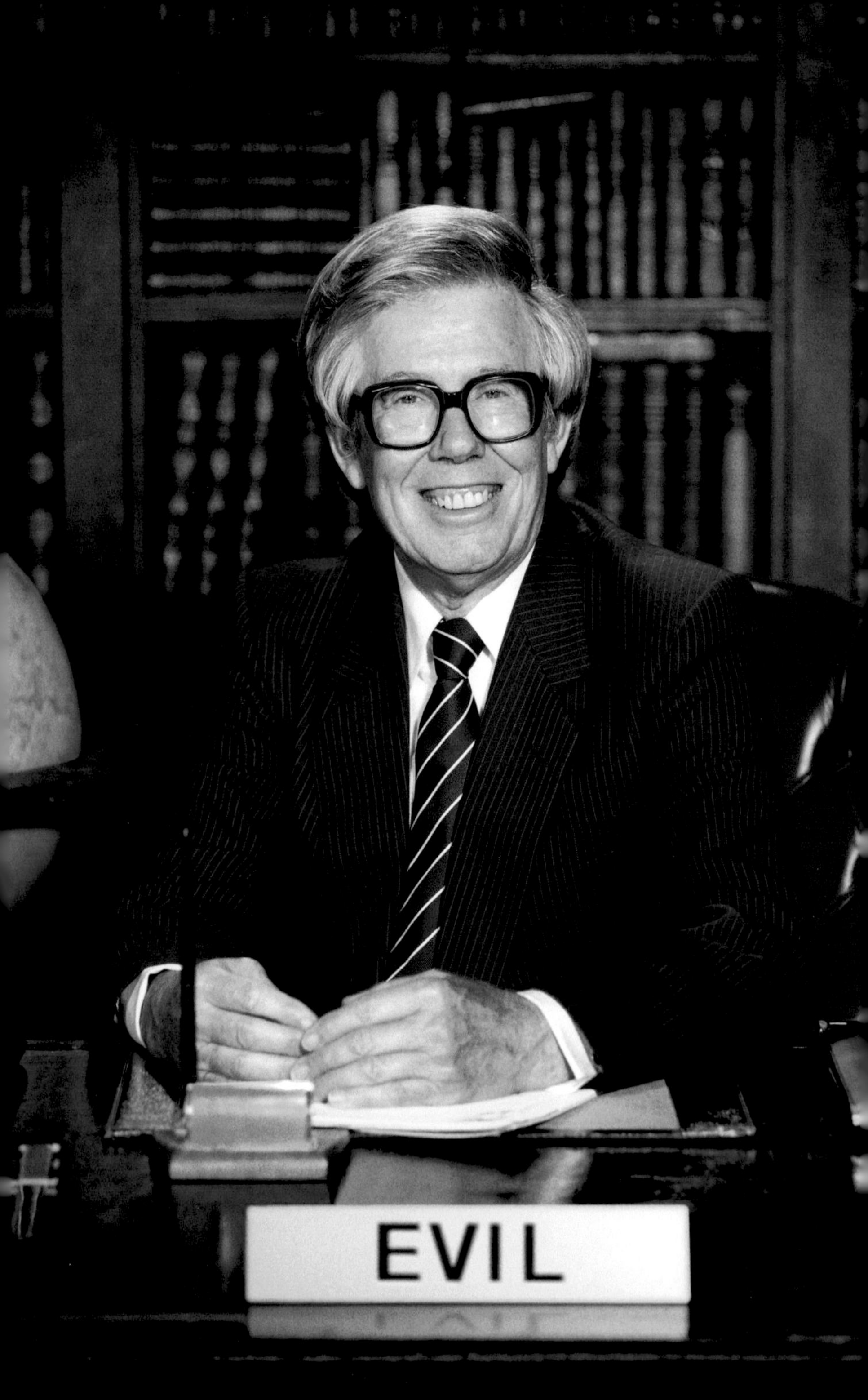
EVIL

cracking name like that, I was itching to ask if I coul
design one for him. He agreed (Oh, joy!) and I couldn'
wait to sink my fangs into it. We decided 'A Larg
Evil Corporation' should appear very large and
very evil. It needed to look like the sort of ruthless
multi-national conglomerate that had its tentacles
in everything; from shipping to petrochemicals
I cast some unlikely looking presidents for its
fictitious worldwide network. I wanted to si
each one of them at their desks behind a menacing
smile and a name plaque that said 'EVIL
Mwahahahaha!! We couldn't afford a photographic
studio so, after everyone had gone home, we sho
them in the small, dank, underground car park
beneath our offices. Obviously we didn't want to
complicate' the process by asking our landlord's
permission. The photographer was my ol' pal Sean
le Sparengo, partnered with the cinematographer
Ben Moulden. Our 'actors' really got into character
exuding *just* the right amount of evil. They were so
good, we shot Super 8 footage too. Enthused by
the results, I kept thinking of new products that

EVIL
THEN SOMEONE SUGGESTED A LARGE EVIL C RPORAT

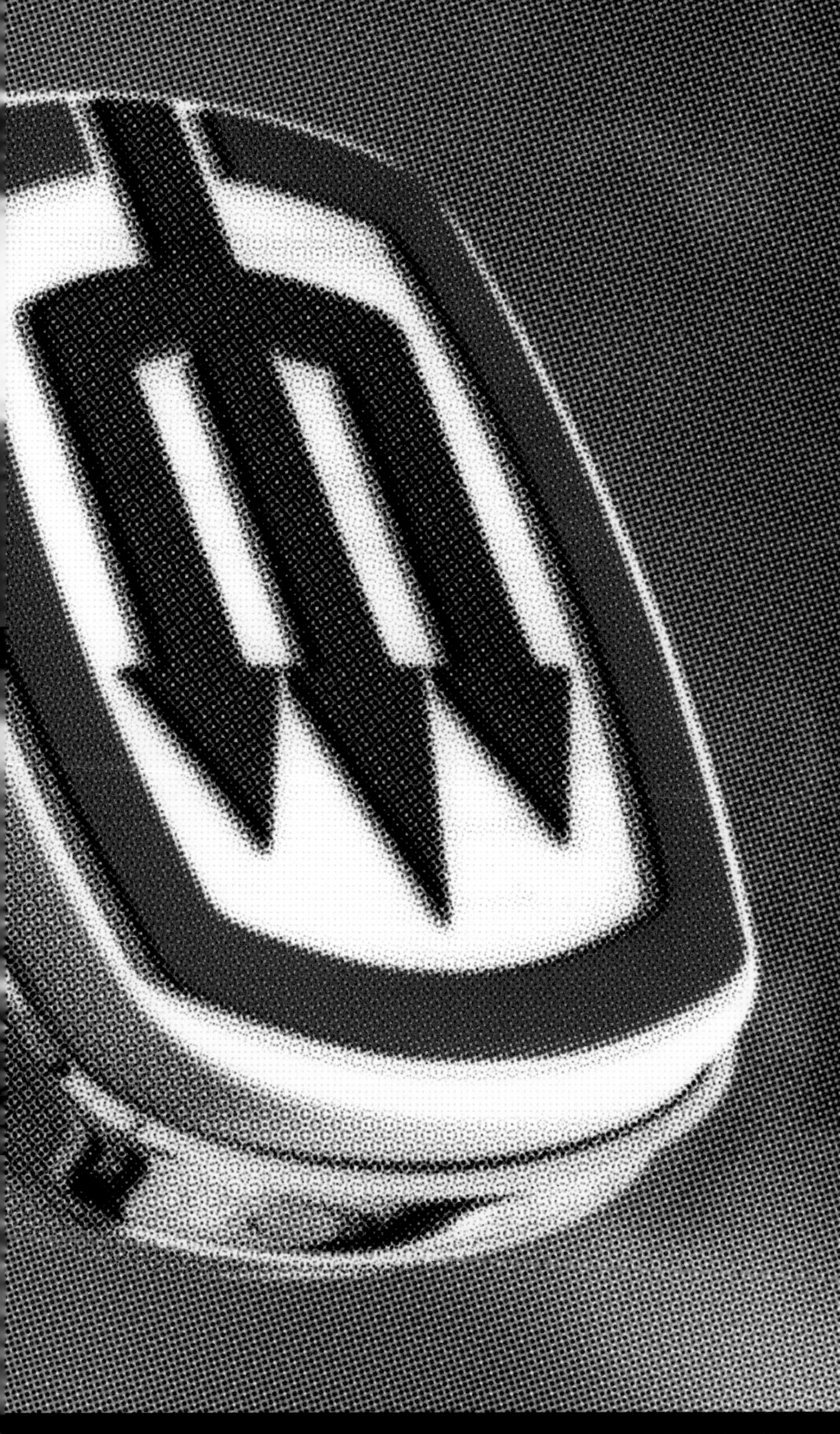

ERYONE LAUGHED. SO THAT'S WHAT WE NAMED THEM.

A Large Evil Corporation might potentially excrete. Evil rolls of wrapping paper for example, featuring a range of bricks with names like 'Beelzebub', 'Diabolos' and 'Satanel'. As for the business cards, what's the root of all evil? Exactly. So I designed cards that looked like dollar bills, bearing pictures of Guy, Seth and A.L.E.C.'s reps, Dara and Ellie. The range of Evil merchandise just kept growing: bags, badges, t-shirts and finally, a magazine. 'Not Nice' magazine was a labour of love and became the perfect vehicle to showcase A Large Evil Corporation's skill in creating C.G. characters. I gave the first issue a 'Fruit & Veg' theme to highlight the nefarious activities down on Evil Farms. Where unnatural foodstuffs were genetically modified alongside 'Farmhouse Bastards' and your choice of gooseberries; 'Rugged' or 'Shaved'. Like Frankenstein's monster, these images soon took on a life of their own with a dedicated exhibition in Soho. Yes, of course there was a party. It was a fantastic night, fuelled by Evil beer which, I can imagine, led to some diabolical hangovers the following morning.

EVIL

HELLO
my name is
EVIL

EVIL

A Large Evil Corporation Ltd, 1 Saville Row, Bath BA1 2QP
Telephone: 01225 46 11 22 Facsimile 01225 46 11 33
www.evilcorp.tv info@evilcorp.tv

WITHOUT COMPLIMENTS

A Large Evil Corporation Ltd, 1 Saville Row, Bath BA1 2QP
Telephone: 01225 46 11 22. Facsimile 01225 46 11 33
www.evilcorp.tv info@evilcorp.tv
Registered in the U.K. No.

# DOING OUR BUSINES

WWW.EVILCORP.TV
Mobile 07765 242 77
guy@evilcorp.tv
Secretary of the Treasury
GUY THOMSON
Director of the Animation
DOING OUR BUSINESS ALL OVER THE WORLD
A LARGE EVIL CORPORATION
THIS NOTE IS EVIL TENDER
FOR ALL DEBTS, PUBLIC AND PRIVATE
+44(0)1225 461 122
WWW.EVILCORP.TV
Mobile 07841 918 28
seth@evilcorp.tv
Director of the Animation
SETH WATKINS
ONE HUNDRED AND ELEVEN PER CENT-24/7
A LARGE EVIL CORPORATION
THIS NOTE IS EVIL TENDER
FOR ALL DEBTS, PUBLIC AND PRIVATE
+44(0)1225 461 122
WWW.EVILCORP.TV
Mobile 07910 020 47
dara@evilcorp.tv
Chief of the Representatives
DARA McDONALD
DOING OUR BUSINESS ALL OVER THE WORLD
A LARGE EVIL CORPORATION
THIS NOTE IS EVIL TENDER
FOR ALL DEBTS, PUBLIC AND PRIVATE
+44(0)1225 461 122
WWW.EVILCORP.TV
Mobile 07841 918 28
seth@evilcorp.tv
LL OVER THE WORLD!

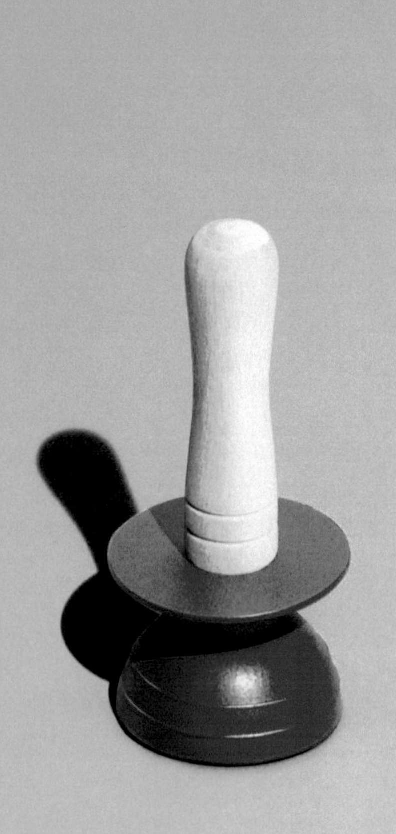

***#2810 Genghis***

***#2811 M***

***#2812 Norman***

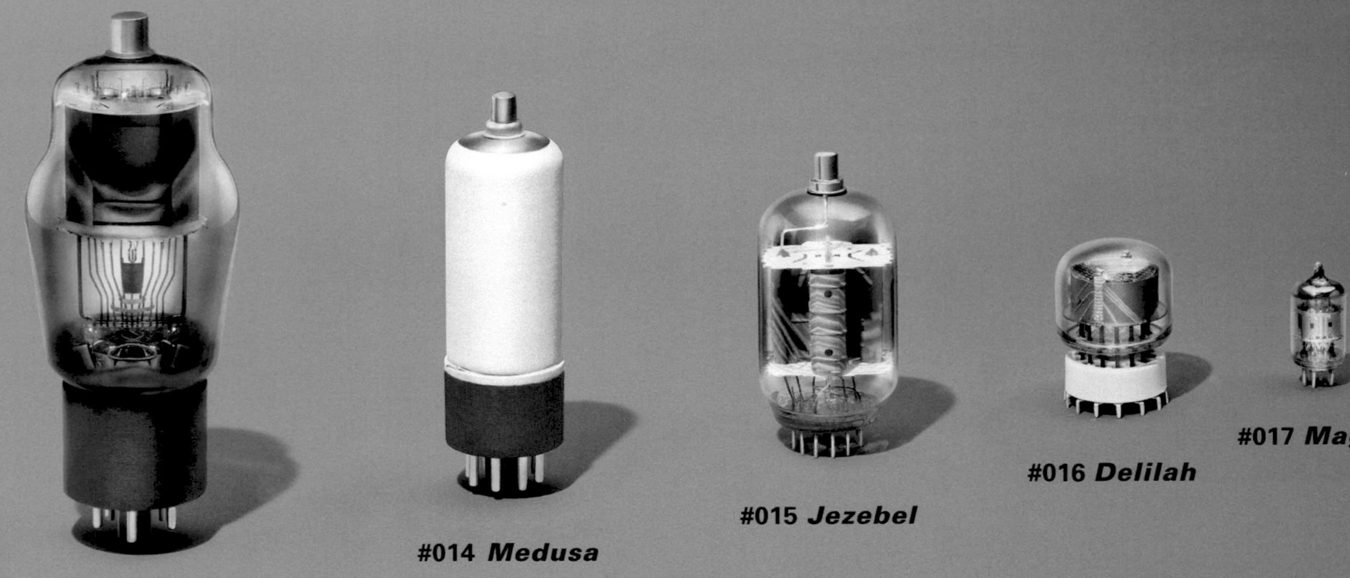
#013 Lucrecia
#014 Medusa
#015 Jezebel

#016 Delilah

#017 Maggie

#1313 Adolf

#1314 Benito
#9787 Wackford
#9786 Attila
#9788 Blakey
#9789 Darth

## #0666 *Imelda*

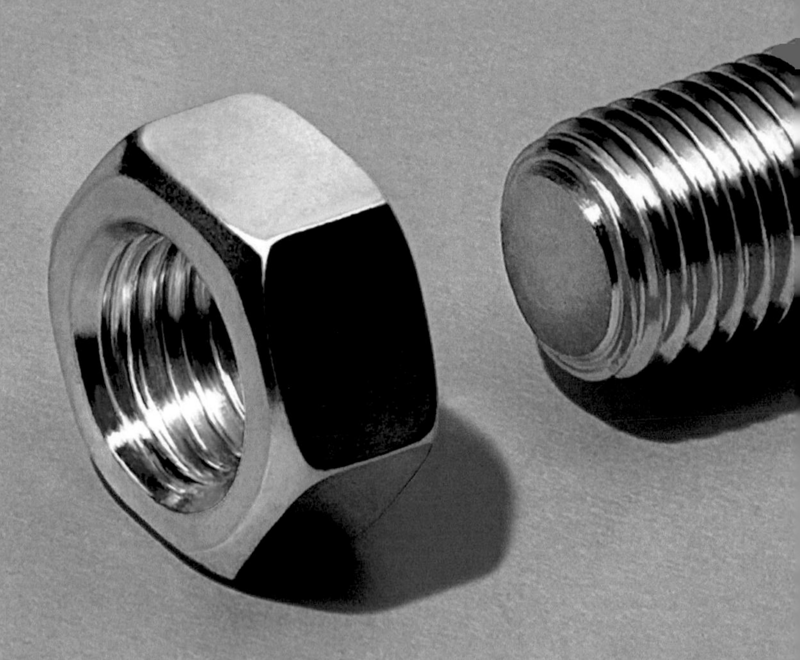

# #0667 *Ferdinand*

**#001** ***Beelzebub***

**#002**

**#009** ***Diabolos***

**#008** ***Black***

# *Their Satanic*

#003 *Mephistopheles*

#004 *The Horned One*

#005 *Azazel*

#006 *Belial*

#007 *Satanel*

EVIL

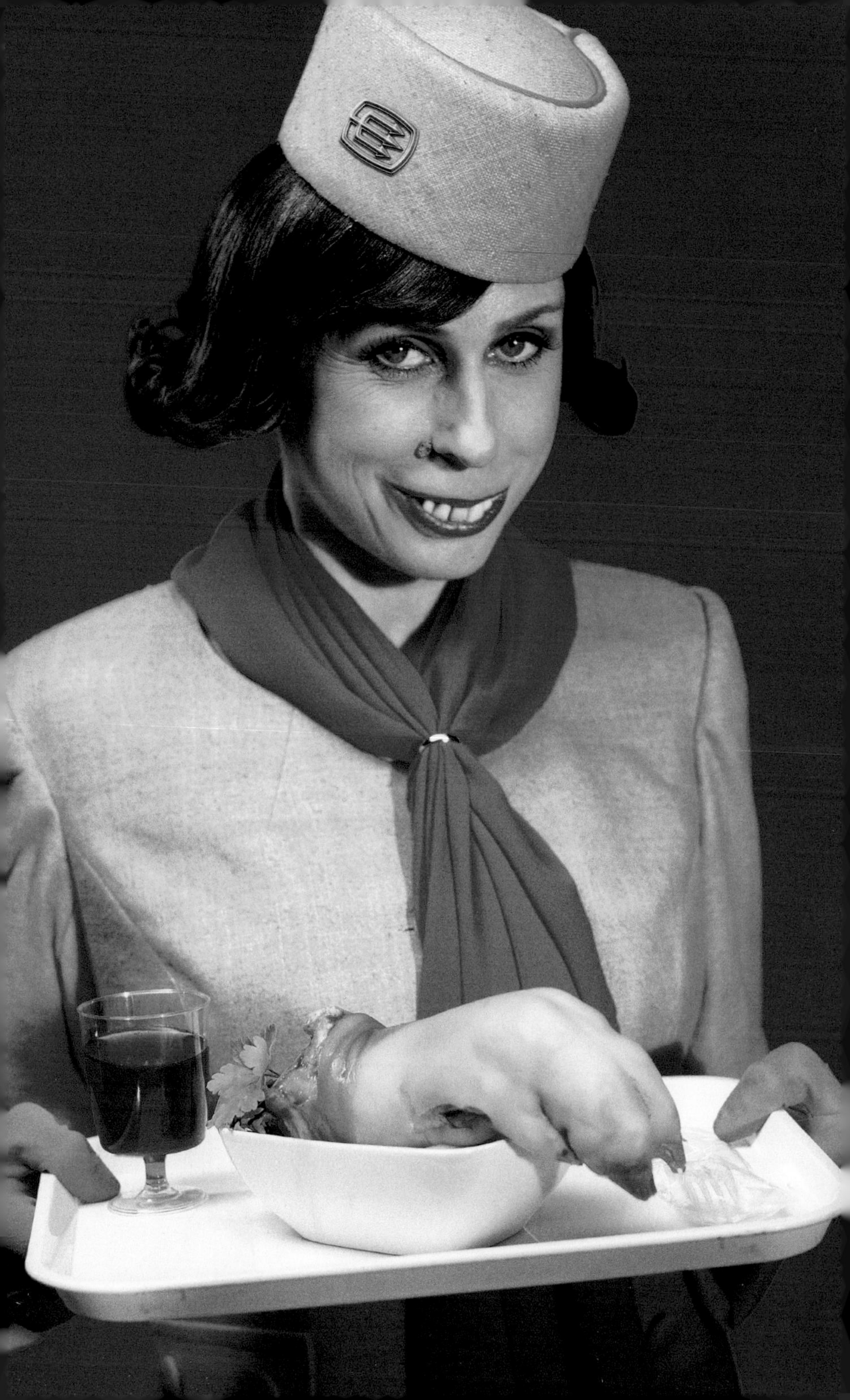

NOT
NICE
WHEN FRUIT AND VEG TURN BAD
№1
THE VITAL ORGAN OF A LARGE EVIL CORPORATION
№1
THE VITAL ORGAN OF A LARGE EVIL CORPORATION

NOT

NICE

ISNICE!

'Not Nice' issue #1 was full of Fra

nstein foods and the like (obys).

Mrs Evil's

BASTARD

IMPORTÉ D'ILFORD

SELECTED ORANGE BEAUTIES
Essex Maiden

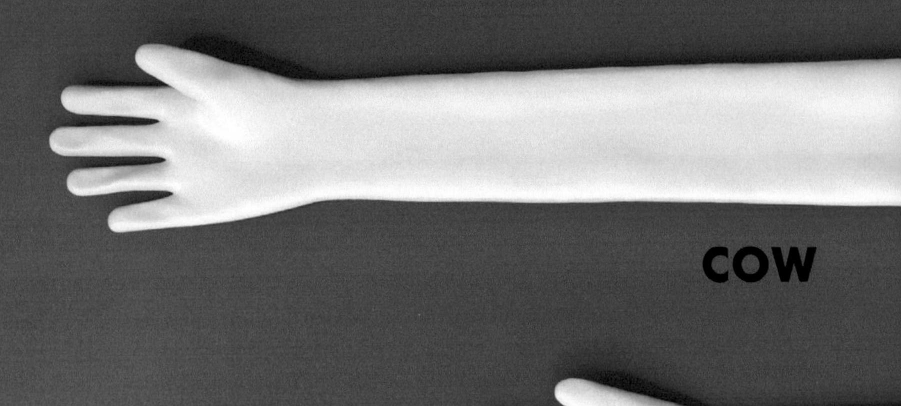

# COW

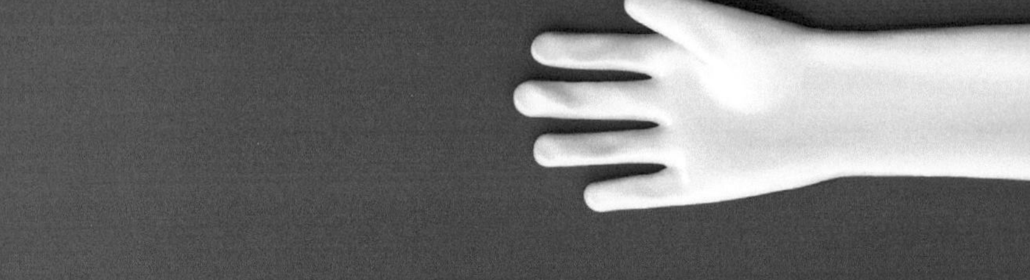

SHEEP

PIG

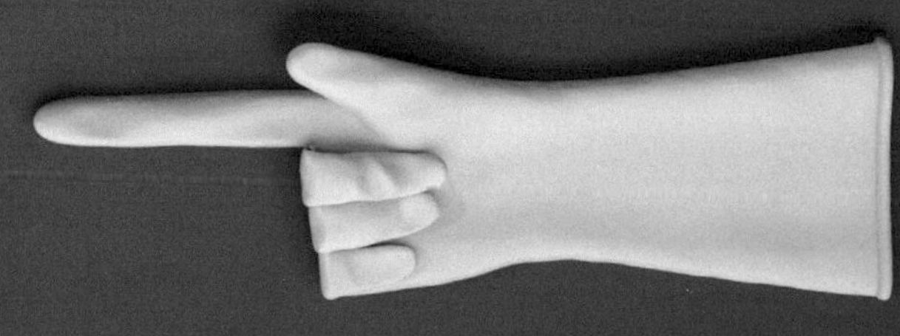

GOOSE

EXTREMELY
BITTER BRAND
LEMONS

Freshly plucked from Evil Farms

(LABORATORIES)

PACKED AND SHIPPED BY
a LARGE EVIL CORPORATION Ltd

MIN NET WT
30 LBS

YOUR "NOT SO LOCAL" INCONVENIENCE STO
OPEN 7 DAYS A WEEK -24/7 (except Wednesday morning, Sunday afternoon, Bank Holidays and ev
Tuesday when our cashier Sandra has her spinning class). Evil Farms Mkt is a subsidiary of A Large Evi
LF-BAKED GOODS
SMELL THE QUALITY!
RRENT BREAD...... £1.50
ST WEEK'S BREAD..... £1.49
UNS OF STEEL ............ PACK 50P
DROPPED SCONES ..........
'PICKED UP' SCONES..........
BIG BAPS .......... TWO FOR
TWO FINGER ROLLS..........
BLOOMER ..........
PAIR OF BLOOMERS ........ EX-
HAM FISTS £2.50 EACH
COLD SHOULDER .......... £1.50 LB
MIDDLE LEG .................. £2 LB
HEFFER LUMPS ........... £3.50 LB
SHREDDED FEET .......... 89P
LIMP BRISKET ............... £1.80 EACH
SMOKED JOINTS .......... £1.50 LB
TICKLED RIBS ............... £3.50 LB
TODAY'S SPECIAL
UNSAVOURY COUNTRY PANCAKES
FRESH* MILK 49P

MILDLY

M

MOVES

MOU

IFFED
TAINS!

There's nothing like a bee in my bonnet to get me buzzing. For example: A few years ago, I was looking through my favourite design book, the D&AD (Designers & Art Directors) annual. It always showcased the best of British design and advertising and had its own unique tone of voice. However, in their latest edition, they'd decided to go international. But in trying to be all things to all markets, they'd lost sight of their original remit and much of their distinctive personality. This made me very sad. I'd been a member of D&AD for decades and had a cherished collection of annuals dating back to 1964. Yet they hadn't consulted me - or any other loyal supporter - about their sudden and unwelcome change of direction. I knew I'd achieve nothing by writing an irate letter. So instead, I turned my attention to the only other British advertising organisation who produced an annual - the Creative Circle. Maybe I could give D&AD a kick up the arse by introducing some healthy competition. I rang up Janice Wilson, who ran the 'Circle', and found out that they

CREATIVE
GOLD

THE CREATIVE CIRCLE
HONOURS 2007 MENU

L'ENTRÉE

POISSONS ET POMMES FRITES
AVEC LES POIS MUSHÈ

LES ACCOMPANIMENTS

LES WALLIES, LES OIGNON5
PRESERVÉS

LES AFTERS

PUDDING DU PAIN & DE
BEURRE, AVEC
CUSTARDE D'OISEAUX

BRITISH ADVERTIS NG'S
B1G NIGHT OUT
MARCH 5TH, 7pM – TO BOOK
CALL 020 7734 9334

were so hard up that they hadn't produced an annual for seven years. As we talked further it transpired that the number of entries to Creative Circle was in steep decline and, out of the Top Ten agencies, seven no longer entered. It was a Catch-22. People almost certainly weren't entering *because* there was no annual. And they couldn't *afford* to produce an annual because there weren't enough entries. Janice asked me if I wanted to be on the committee. I took a deep breath, swallowed hard and said, "Only if I can be President." In return, I promised I'd produce an annual for them. They had nothing to lose and plenty to gain so, like some dodgy dictator, I was declared President without an election. The first task was to change the logo which, for obvious reasons, had always been a circle. But I thought a square would actually be a far more *creative* circle. And what about square trophies too? Especially if I could get them made by the same company who'd made the original FA Cup. Before I could do all that though, I had to find some cash. Not much, just enough to get the wheels turning. The Circle had no sponsors, so I had to pick up the phone and start calling companies who might be interested. In exchange for their lolly, I offered each of them a print ad in the new annual, which I promised would be written by a great creative team. The only caveat - the team in question would be allowed a completely free hand. So the sponsors got some fantastic work from some seriously talented writers and art directors. And those teams, in turn, got the rare chance to produce an ad with absolutely zero interference from the client. The money soon began to pour in and we could start making the trophies and designing the annual. The President was, of course, desperate to design it himself but suddenly he thought, "NO!" Unlike D&AD, who'd seemingly abandoned their whole purpose without consulting anyone, the Creative Circle was a very inclusive organisation. It belonged to the creative community, so I approached the brilliant Paul Belford to design the annual. Paul's work has a minimalist sophistication

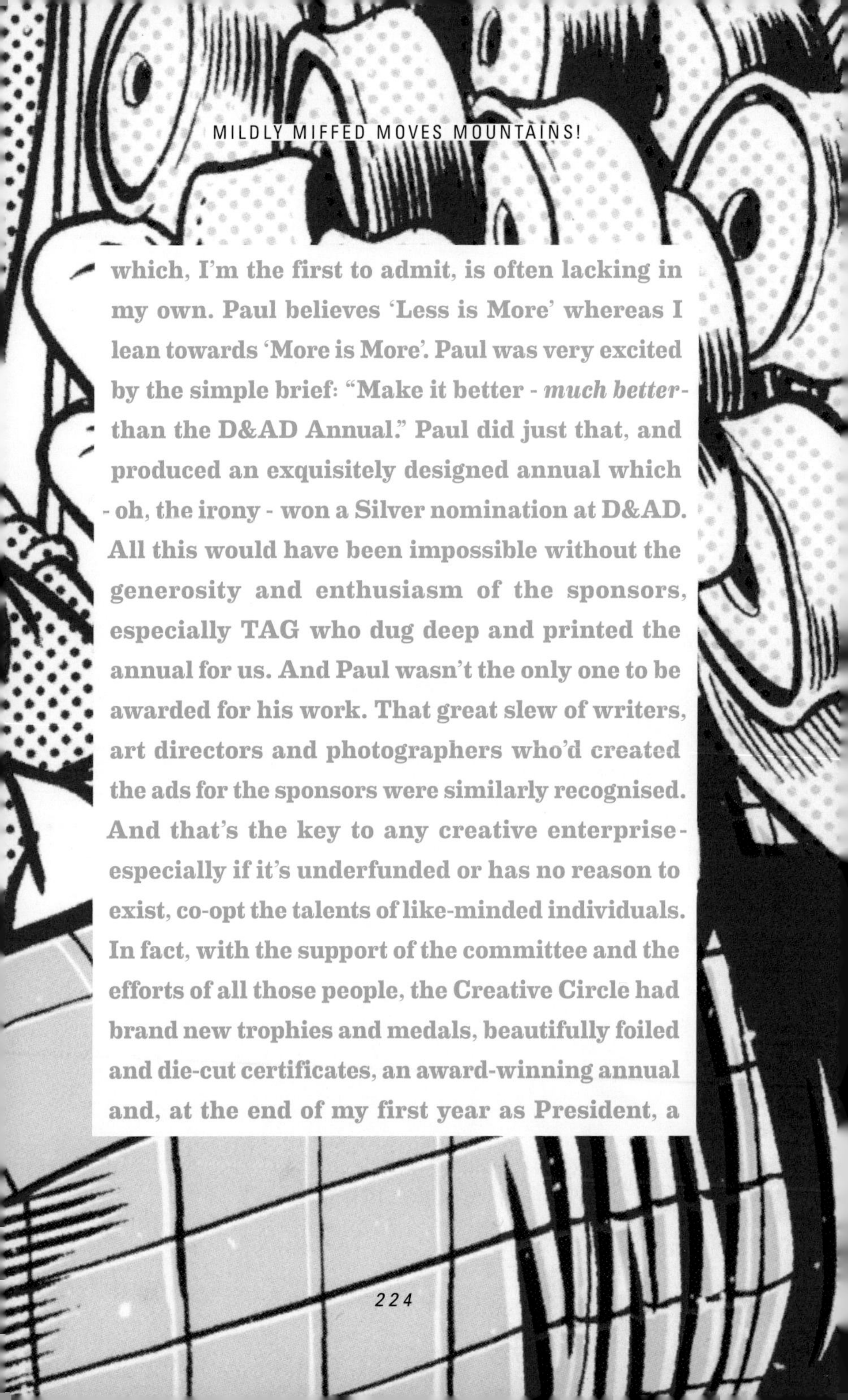

which, I'm the first to admit, is often lacking in my own. Paul believes 'Less is More' whereas I lean towards 'More is More'. Paul was very excited by the simple brief: "Make it better - *much better* - than the D&AD Annual." Paul did just that, and produced an exquisitely designed annual which - oh, the irony - won a Silver nomination at D&AD. All this would have been impossible without the generosity and enthusiasm of the sponsors, especially TAG who dug deep and printed the annual for us. And Paul wasn't the only one to be awarded for his work. That great slew of writers, art directors and photographers who'd created the ads for the sponsors were similarly recognised. And that's the key to any creative enterprise - especially if it's underfunded or has no reason to exist, co-opt the talents of like-minded individuals. In fact, with the support of the committee and the efforts of all those people, the Creative Circle had brand new trophies and medals, beautifully foiled and die-cut certificates, an award-winning annual and, at the end of my first year as President, a

CIRCLE
CIRCLE

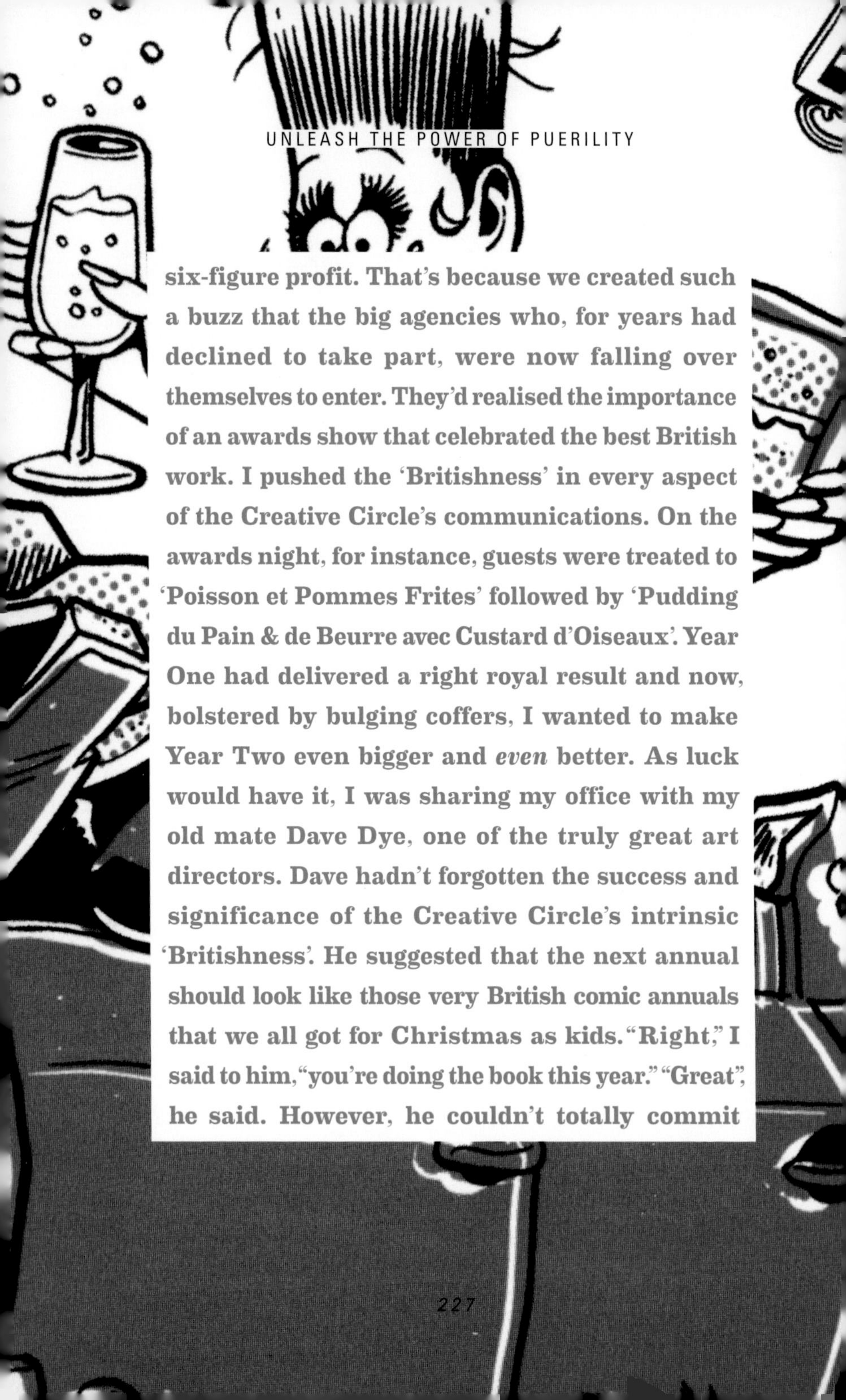



six-figure profit. That's because we created such a buzz that the big agencies who, for years had declined to take part, were now falling over themselves to enter. They'd realised the importance of an awards show that celebrated the best British work. I pushed the 'Britishness' in every aspect of the Creative Circle's communications. On the awards night, for instance, guests were treated to 'Poisson et Pommes Frites' followed by 'Pudding du Pain & de Beurre avec Custard d'Oiseaux'. Year One had delivered a right royal result and now, bolstered by bulging coffers, I wanted to make Year Two even bigger and *even* better. As luck would have it, I was sharing my office with my old mate Dave Dye, one of the truly great art directors. Dave hadn't forgotten the success and significance of the Creative Circle's intrinsic 'Britishness'. He suggested that the next annual should look like those very British comic annuals that we all got for Christmas as kids. "Right," I said to him, "you're doing the book this year." "Great", he said. However, he couldn't totally commit

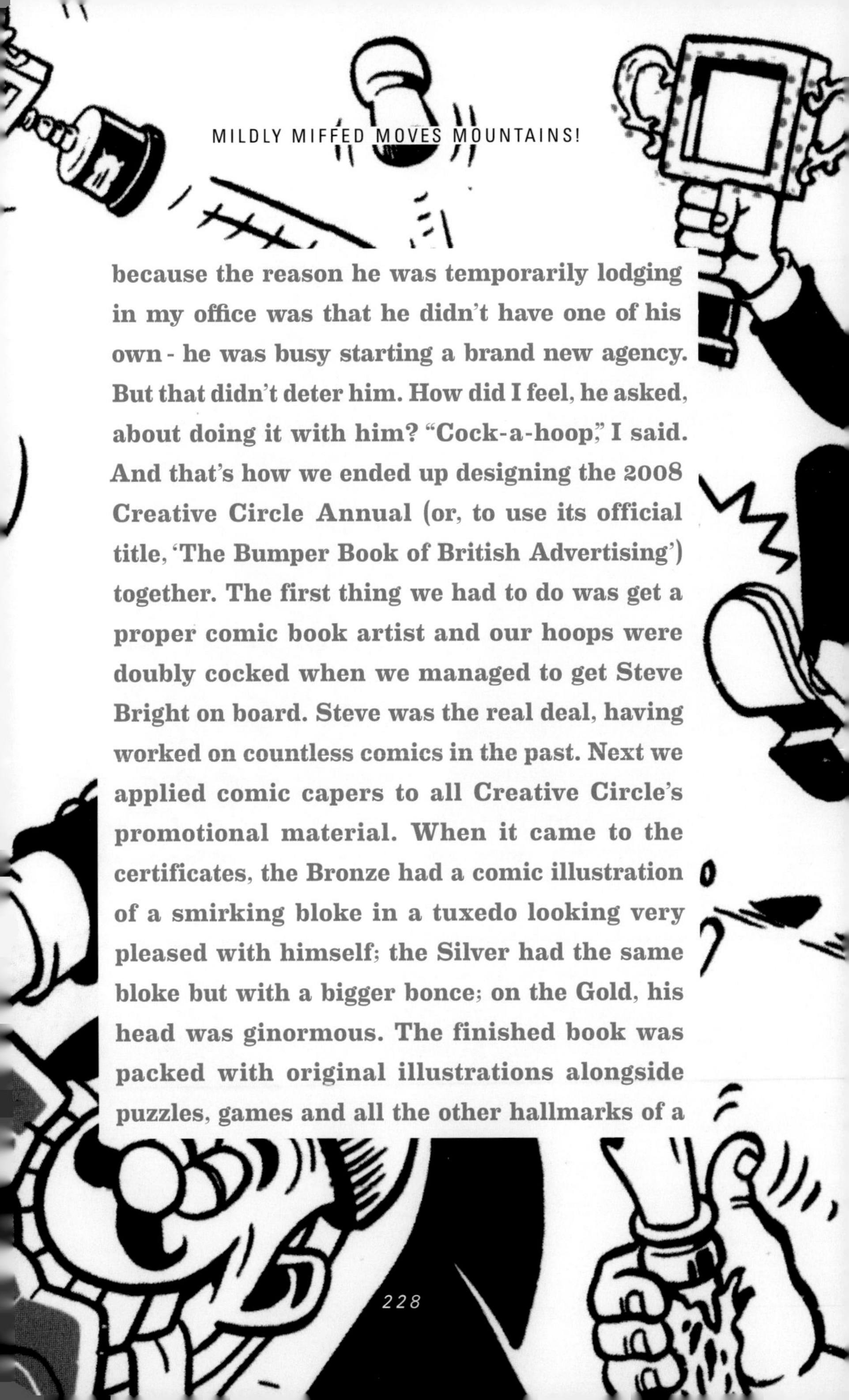



because the reason he was temporarily lodging in my office was that he didn't have one of his own - he was busy starting a brand new agency. But that didn't deter him. How did I feel, he asked, about doing it with him? "Cock-a-hoop," I said. And that's how we ended up designing the 2008 Creative Circle Annual (or, to use its official title, 'The Bumper Book of British Advertising') together. The first thing we had to do was get a proper comic book artist and our hoops were doubly cocked when we managed to get Steve Bright on board. Steve was the real deal, having worked on countless comics in the past. Next we applied comic capers to all Creative Circle's promotional material. When it came to the certificates, the Bronze had a comic illustration of a smirking bloke in a tuxedo looking very pleased with himself; the Silver had the same bloke but with a bigger bonce; on the Gold, his head was ginormous. The finished book was packed with original illustrations alongside puzzles, games and all the other hallmarks of a

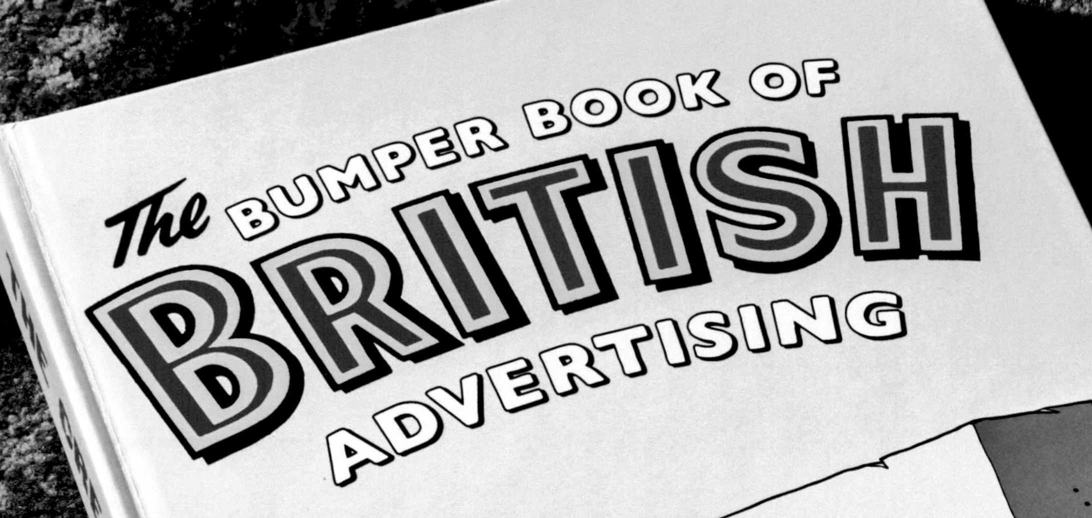

The BUMPER BOOK OF
BRITISH
ADVERTISING

CIRCLE
ANNUAL 2008

great comic annual but with an advertising theme. It was also chock-full of fabulous ads because Year Two had attracted even more entries than Year One. And again, the annual won a D&AD Silver nomination. As our comic book characters might say, "Tee-hee!" How on earth would we follow that for Year Three? Filled with optimism, we'd just begun to think about how we would design the new annual when the global financial crisis happened. The first casualty of ad agency belt-tightening is always awards budgets. However, within every crisis, there's an opportunity. We just had to find it. Pronto. We decided we needed to be honest about the financial situation and reflect it in what we did. So the 2009 Creative Circle 'Call for Entries' became the 2009 Creative Circle '*Plea for Entries*'. I enlisted my talented and gloriously monikered stepdaughter, Saskia Laroque Rothstein-Longaretti, to re-fashion the trophy and medals in silver and gold baking foil. The '*Plea for Entries*' mailers were lashed together from cardboard,

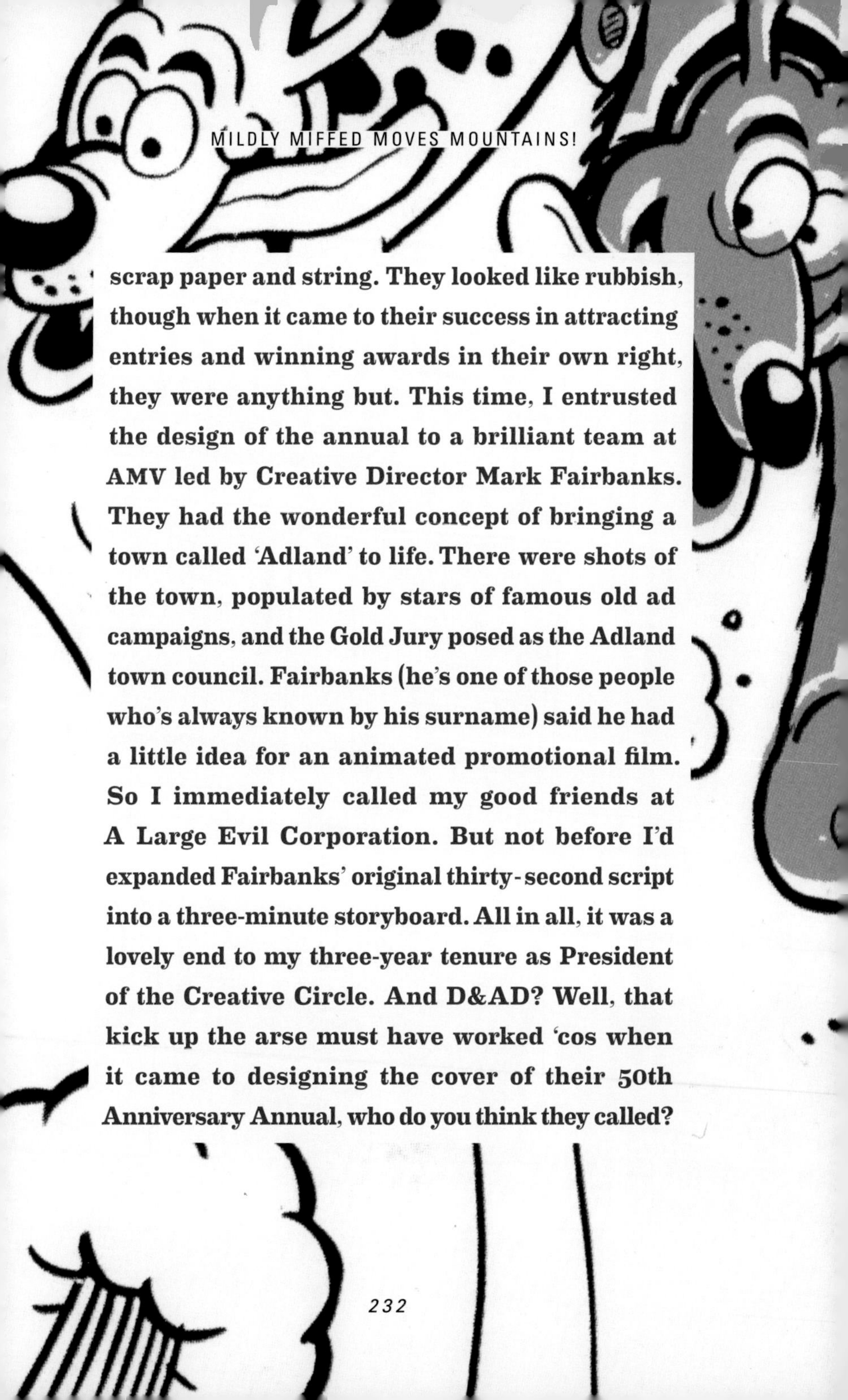

scrap paper and string. They looked like rubbish, though when it came to their success in attracting entries and winning awards in their own right, they were anything but. This time, I entrusted the design of the annual to a brilliant team at AMV led by Creative Director Mark Fairbanks. They had the wonderful concept of bringing a town called 'Adland' to life. There were shots of the town, populated by stars of famous old ad campaigns, and the Gold Jury posed as the Adland town council. Fairbanks (he's one of those people who's always known by his surname) said he had a little idea for an animated promotional film. So I immediately called my good friends at A Large Evil Corporation. But not before I'd expanded Fairbanks' original thirty-second script into a three-minute storyboard. All in all, it was a lovely end to my three-year tenure as President of the Creative Circle. And D&AD? Well, that kick up the arse must have worked 'cos when it came to designing the cover of their 50th Anniversary Annual, who do you think they called?

*The Creative Circle used to be iffy—*

The PRESIDENT'S STATEMENT!
Mark Denton esq.

THIS INTERNATIONAL DESIGN AND ADVERTISING BOOK'S A BIT IMPENETRABLE
INTERNATIONAL AWARDS
INTERNATIONAL ANNUAL OF GRAPHIC DESIGN, ADVERTISING, ARCHITECTURE, BOOKS, MAGAZINES, WEBSITE DESIGN, TV TITLES, SHELF WOBBLERS, FORKLIFT TRUCKS, PANTYHOSE PACKAGING, POP PROMOS, SHOP FRONTS,

I DON'T CARE WHO WON GOLD FOR SWEDISH FORKLIFT TRUCK DESIGN!
GOLD

EXCELENTÉ
PANCHO'S PAPER CLIPS
I WONDER IF THIS MEXICAN 96-SHEET CAMPAIGN FOR PAPER CLIPS EVER ACTUALLY RAN?

IDEA

*— now it's good, thanks t'Commitee!*

LATER –
........ IS THAT THE CREATIVE CIRCLE? ...........WOULD YOU BE INTERESTED IN CHANGING ALL YOUR CATEGORIES, UPGRADING YOUR JURIES, REDESIGNING YOUR IDENTITY, HIRING THE FIRM THAT MADE THE F.A. CUP TO MAKE NEW TROPHIES AND MEDALS, AND HONOURING PAUL ARDEN & DAVID ABBOTT WITH A NEW AWARD CALLED THE HALL OF HEROES? HOW ABOUT RELAUNCHING THE CREATIVE CIRCLE ANNUAL AND ASKING PAUL BELFORD TO DESIGN IT? THEN ASKING PAUL SILBURN, DAVE DYE AND JERRY GALLAHER TO SIT ON THE COMMITTEE, ESTABLISHING A NEW DIGITAL SECTION, AND SORTING OUT A DVD OF THE YEAR'S WINNERS, AND RESTARTING THE MEMBERSHIP....... OH, AND THE ROLE REVERSAL SEMINAR COULD DO WITH A REBRAND. OBVIOUSLY YOU'RE GOING TO NEED LOADS OF LOVELY NEW SPONSORS TO HELP MAKE IT HAPPEN ..... AND WHILE YOU'RE AT IT YOU'LL HAVE TO GET RID OF YOUR INTERNATIONAL BIT BECAUSE IT'S REALLY GOT TO BE ABOUT THE BEST OF OF BRITISH ADVERTISING......
.....YOU'RE ON FOR IT? BRILLIANT!
JOY
GREAT......... I THINK IT'S TIME FOR A COOL MEAT PIE AND A LIE-DOWN
...OF COURSE I COULDN'T HAVE DONE IT WITHOUT THE HELP AND SUPPORT OF THE COMMITTEE – MANY THANKS TO :– RICK BRIM, DAVE DYE, JERRY GALLAHER, MALCOLM GASKIN, TONY HARDCASTLE, OWEN LEE, MIKE MCKENNA, PAUL SHEARER, PAUL SILBURN AND BRENDAN WILKINS

YIKES! WE'RE ABOUT TO START PRINTING 'THE BUMPER BOOK OF BRITISH ADVERTISING', SO WE NEED SOME BRITISH ADVERTISING TO PUT IN IT. IF YOU WANT IT TO BE YOURS, WITH YOUR NAME UNDERNEATH, JUST GO TO CREATIVECIRCLE.CO.UK OR PHONE 020 7734 9334 FOR DETAILS.
CALL

LOLLY
CONCEPT: DAVE DYE AND MARK DENTON · AGENCY: LYE HOLLOWAY MURRAY · COPY: DAVE DYE · TYPOGRAPHY: ANDY DYMOCK · DESIGN: MARK DENTON DESIGN · PROUDLY PRINTED IN ENGLAND

TUCK IN TO THE BEST OF ADVERTISING – THE CREATIVE CIRCLE BIG BASH 2008. FILL YOUR FACE WITH BANGERS 'N' MASH, SPOTTED DICK 'N' CUSTARD AND CHORTLE ALONG TO JIMMY CARR. MARCH 3RD 7PM TILL SILLY O'CLOCK. TO BOOK CALL 020 7734 9334.

PICK UP YOUR COPY OF THE ~~LONG OVERDUE~~, EAGERLY AWAITED 2008 CREATIVE
CIRCLE ANNUAL AT THE OFFICIAL LAUNCH - WEDNESDAY 28TH JANUARY. JUST GO
TO CREATIVECIRCLE.CO.UK OR PHONE 020 7734 9334 FOR DETAILS.
THE CREATIVE CIRCLE ANNUAL 2008
CREATIVE CIRCLE
THE CREATIVE CIRCLE ANNUAL 2008
CREATIVE CIRCLE

# DEATH by 1,000 CUTS

This is the game of getting a T.V. commercial on air. All you need is 2 players, a dice ......Oh, and the best of British luck!

T.V. AND CINEMA!
EAT MORE PIES!

SERVICE the CLIENT
A.
B.
C.
OUR INTREPID ACCOUNT MAN CAN'T FIND A WA
TO PLEASE THE CLIENT! — CAN YOU HELP?

EAT MORE PIES!
Radio

My name is Therapy Films - Viral Therapy
From Mark Denton Design I've won a
CERTIFICATE
in the Best Illustration Category
My name is Andy Dymock Viral Therapy
From Dymock I've won a
BRONZE
in the Best Illustration Category

The
BUMPER DVD OF
BRITISH
ADVERTISING

My name is MTV - Characters
From This is Real Art I've won a
SILVER
in the Best Prog. Sponsorship/Idents Category

My name is To Not Advertise Here
From Saatchi & Saatchi I've won a
GOLD
in the Best Trade Advertisement Category

BIG BASH!
MONDA
3 MARC
7pm-2a
200

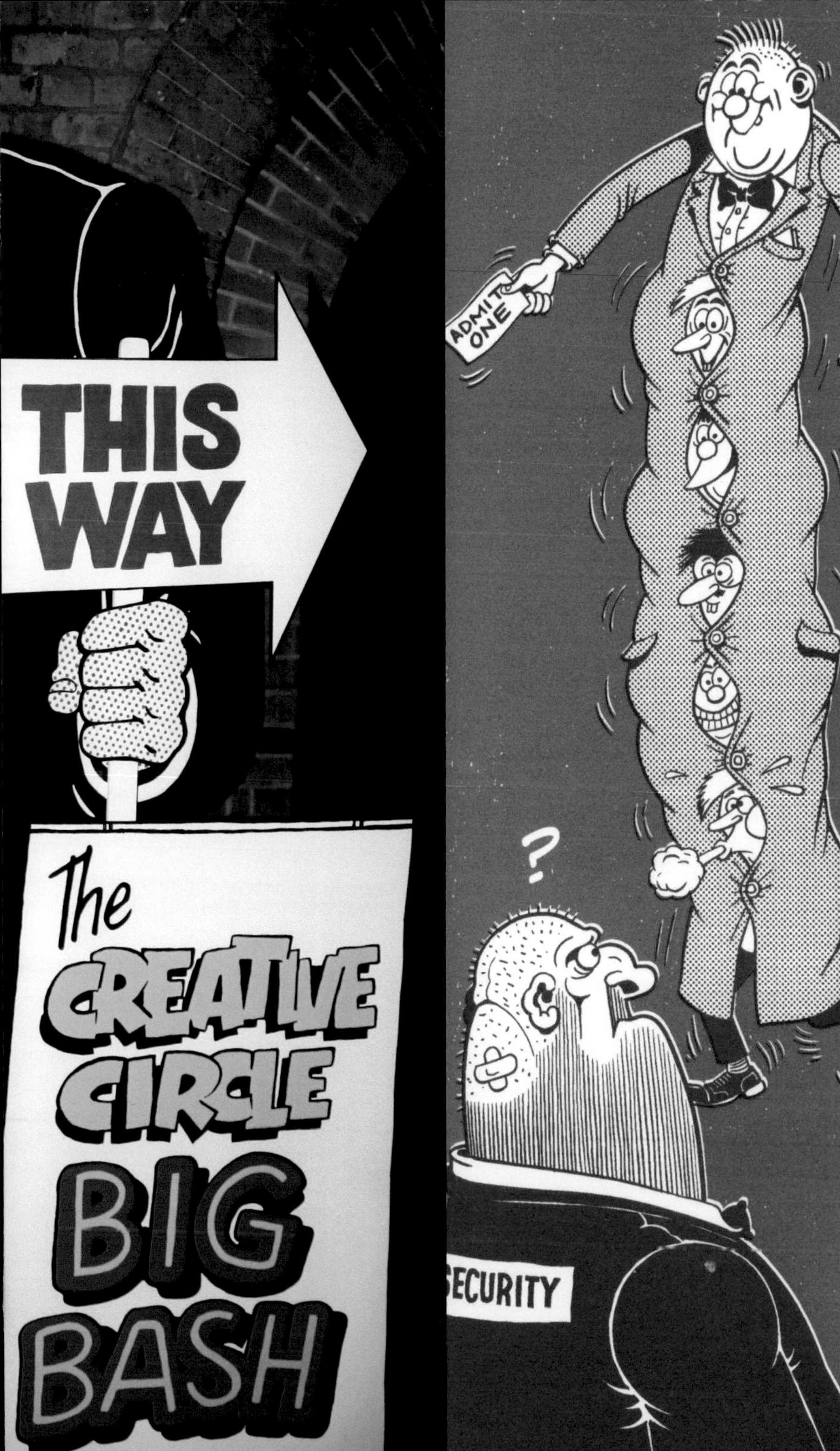
THIS WAY
The CREATIVE CIRCLE BIG BASH
ADMIT ONE
?
SECURITY

THEN ALONG CAME

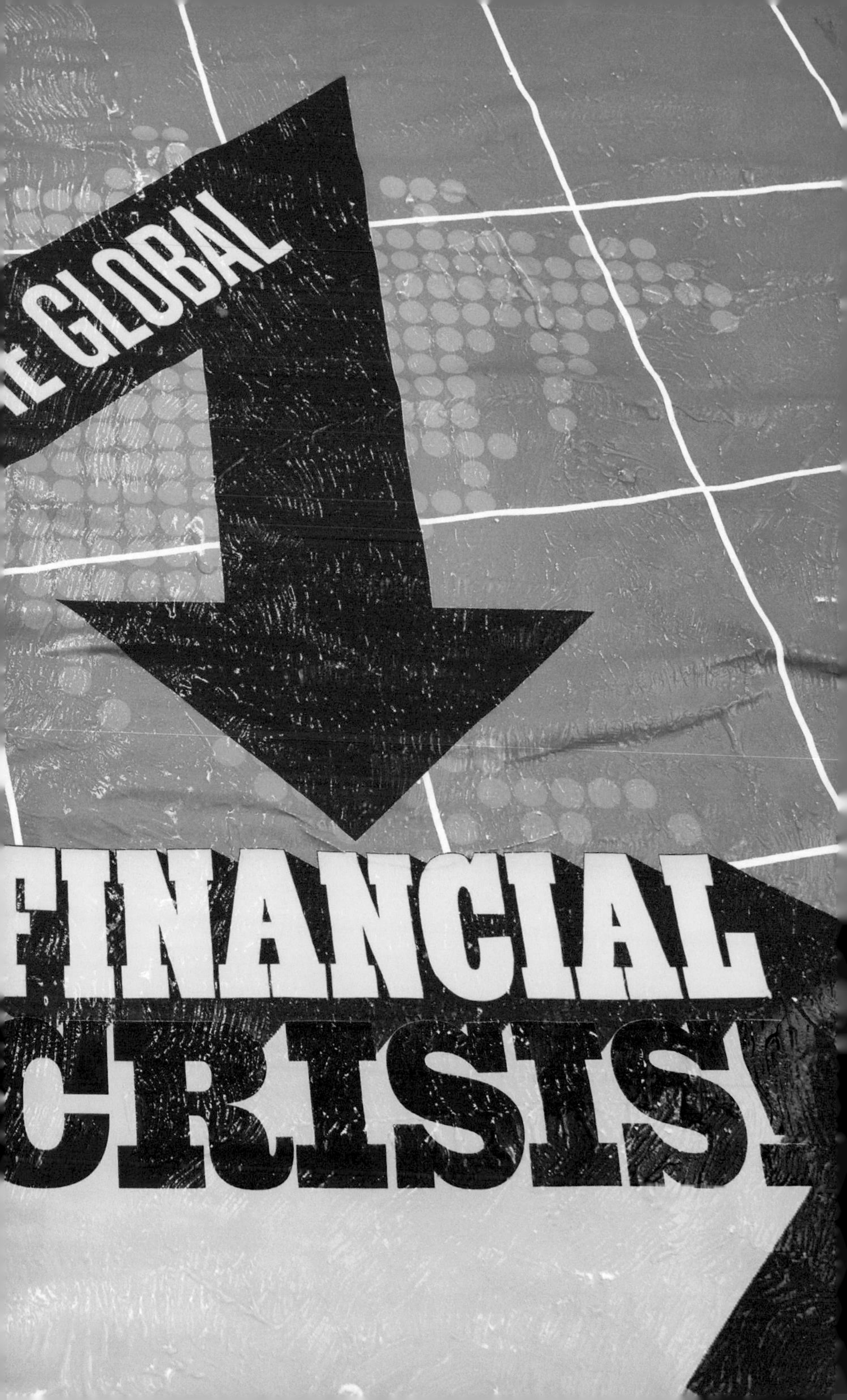

GLOBAL

FINANCIAL

CRISIS

THE 2009 'PLEA FOR ENTRIES' LOOKED LIKE RUBBI

RY *VERY* EXPENSIVE SCREEN-PRINTED RUBBISH...

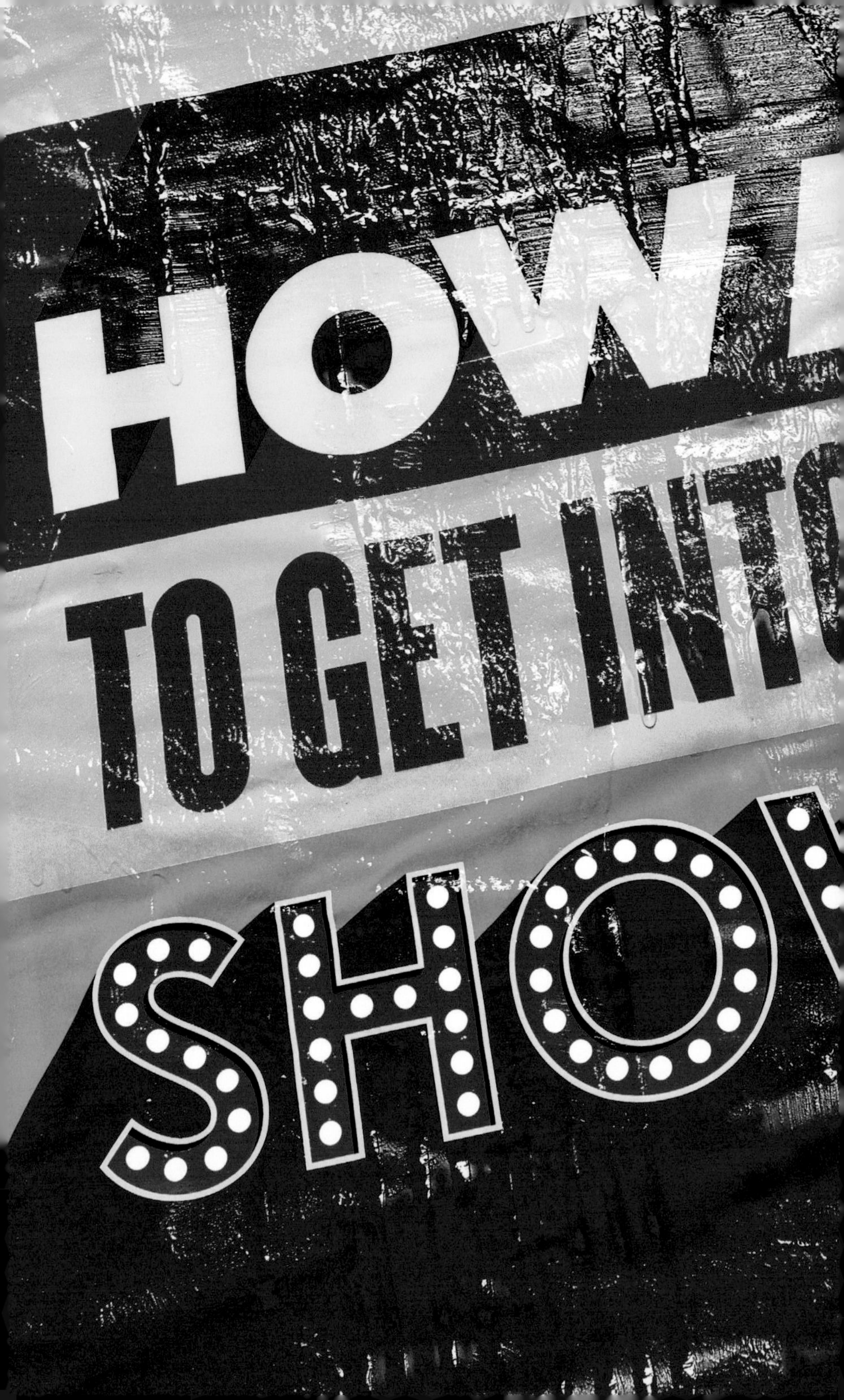
HOW
TO GET INT
SHO

V BIZ!

**I met my lovely wife Anna on the set of a commercial about 25 years ago. She was a beautiful and, well, quite 'vocal' hair and make-up artist. But my God, she was good. Really knew her chignons. Working together led to going out together and, a few years later, to getting married. I'd barely carried her over the threshold when she announced, "I don't want to do hair and make-up any more. I want to be a writer." If I'd still been carrying her, I might have dropped her. Instead it was only my jaw that dropped. "What do you mean you want to be a writer?" I said. "Which part of that sentence don't you understand?" she replied. Told you she was 'vocal'. But when Anna decides to do something, she does it properly. So she enrolled on a screenwriting course, a filmmaking course, acting courses and stand-up comedy courses. When she wasn't on a course, she was reading. And when she wasn't reading, she was writing. Her first full-length film script was a coming-of-age story set in the skinhead era of 1969.**

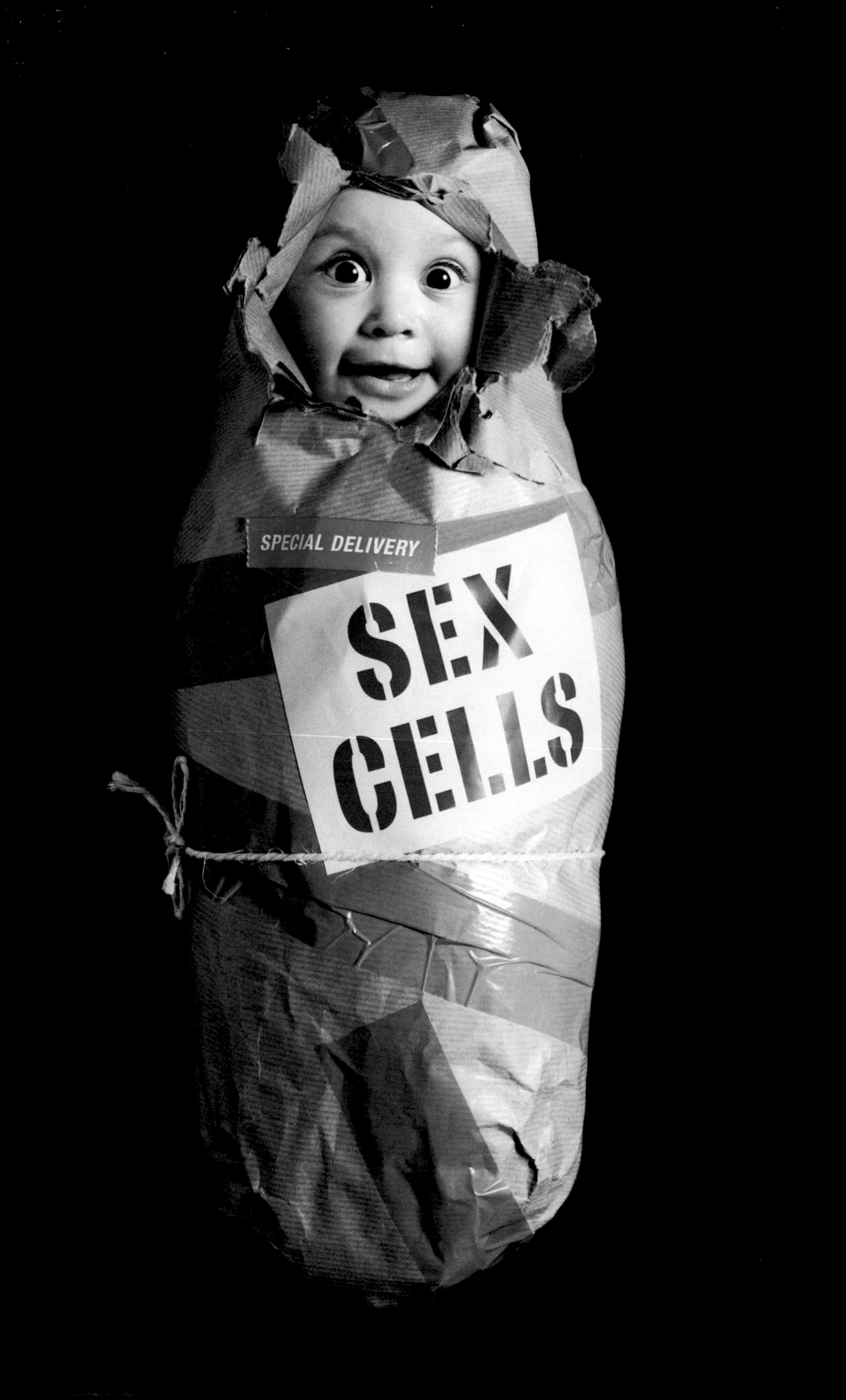

SPECIAL DELIVERY

SEX CELLS

FRAGILE
FRAGILE

I loved it, not just because of the funny, authentic dialogue and engaging characters, but also because in '69, I became a teenager and it brought back some very happy crop-haired memories. Her second was about an old taxi driver who unwittingly gets involved in a murky world of international crime. His life becomes entangled with that of a young, insanely handsome ex-model. Although they are polar opposites, their lives turn out to be surprisingly similar. I thought both were brilliant scripts but after they were finished, we looked at each other and thought, "What now?" How do you get a script in front of the people with the know-how to get it made? Being in our fifties, we simply didn't have the time, or - let's be honest - the patience to find out. So we decided to put on a play instead, thinking, 'How hard can it be?' Hmm, we often have a chuckle about that. Anna set about writing a brand new script. "We can't put those film scripts on stage," she explained, "because film writing is visual and play writing is...

it's... *wordual.*" She's a regular theatre-goer, so she knows what she's talking about, and sometimes drags me along if she thinks I could do with a kip. Sometimes I leave at half-time; especially if the actors start shouting at each other. Her play was set in a call centre that sells sex toys but, despite that (and being called '*Sex Cells*') it wasn't very sexy. It featured four women, each with very different attitudes towards motherhood, and their beleaguered manager. I say 'manager' because he definitely wasn't their boss. When Anna described it to me, I baulked. A play about *motherhood*? I was rummaging for words to let her down gently, terms like 'interesting' or 'challenging'. But when I started reading it, I kept getting interrupted by the sound of some bloke laughing uproariously. After a bit, I realised the noise was coming from me. It was so good. Very moving and very funny. A bit like life, really. "This has to be seen!" I pronounced grandly, "Let's hire a West End theatre." Anna looked into it and informed me that it would cost the price of a house. At least now we knew why a theatre was called a 'house'. "Could you get a producer and director to help us?" I asked. And, after enquiries were made, "No-one's interested," she sighed. "What if we funded it ourselves?" I said, "Could we get one then?" "Yes!" She rallied, "I've found a bus driver who gets a bit theatrical in his spare time!" Alarm bells were ringing but we had no other choice, since neither of us had the foggiest about theatre production. Unsurprisingly, Anna and the bus driver had 'creative differences'. Mainly over his insistence - and her refusal - to write in a male character who wore hot pants. They parted company. However, since being 'vocal' is an ideal quality in a theatre producer, she took on the job herself. We booked The Riverside Studios in Hammersmith for a month-long run, rehearsals began and then it dawned on us... a month?? We had to fill 240 seats, eight times a week, for a *month*. We'd have to find an audience of *thousands*. How on earth do you raise

# "MY SHOW WILL GO ON"

## ON PRODUCING MY OWN PLAY

I'm not a theatre producer, I know nothing about producing theatre - I've never even been in a professional play. I didn't want to do it, and I'm not sure I'll ever do it again. That being said, it felt like the forces of nature led me here. I'm not sure if it was self-belief or sheer belligerence that got me to this point — a four-week run of my debut play at Riverside Studios. I ask myself everyday if I am mad. I have been politely turned down by theatres and producers, (though to be fair, I didn't manage to get in front of many producers.) Happily, there were enough people who believed in this play (and me) to keep me going. The process has been eye-opening. I've learned a lot about how the theatre works. I've been given advice from lots of people on how it's done, and I'd like to thank everyone who offered it. For the most part I have taken that advice gratefully, but I've also done things that felt right for me and sometimes challenged the norm. I've no one to blame for the success or failure of this project because, as the song says: 'I did it my way'.

awareness of something and then get people to *buy* it? Oh yeah. Of course. You do the thing I've spent my entire working life doing: you *advertise*. But this time it felt different. This was a product - and a client - that were personally important to me. Not that every client isn't hugely important but, you know what I mean. I wrote a little trailer, which went down very well and then thought, "Who's really good at advertising?" I rang Dave Dye. With the help of Posterscope we secured a digital super-site on Hammersmith roundabout, and Dave created a brilliant campaign to put on it. I particularly loved the endline: '*Coming to a Theatre Near You* [if you live in the Hammersmith area]'. Now, for the programme. The theatre staff said we'd be lucky if we could charge as much as three quid for 'em and we'd never shift more than fifty. But what if it was more interesting than your average programme, filled with original content? I'm happy to report that we sold more than fifty and charged a fiver 'dahling!' There was now nothing more I could do except sit nervously in my seat as the curtain went up. Showtime! We had to learn the difference between 'Opening night', 'First night' and 'Press night', but I was glued to the seat for all of them and watched the attendance increase as the run progressed. I got to witness people laughing one minute and crying the next. And I mean really *crying*. I saw a whole row of shaking shoulders as a party of women in front of me sobbed in unison. Unseen behind them, I was sobbing too. Anna had put so much effort, love, heart and soul into this project, that, like most artistes, she was terrified that the critics would tear it to shreds. She'd turned into a quivering, nail-biting wreck. She needn't have worried though. The critics and audiences absolutely LOVED it. She stopped shaking, grew all her nails back and I got my lovely missus back too. In between bouts of sobbing in the stalls, I kept thinking: "But what's going to happen once the run has ended?" (See how quickly I picked up the lingo?) "Will we have to

M25
DELAY
SPRAY
24 GIANT SIZE PKGS

M25
DELAY
SPRAY
24 GIANT SIZE PKGS

M25
DELAY
SPRAY
24 GIANT SIZE PKGS

M25
DELAY
SPRAY
24 GIANT SIZE PKGS

M25
DELAY
SPRAY
24 GIANT SIZE PKGS

M25
DELAY
SPRAY
24 GIANT SIZE PKGS

TITIVATORS

20 PKS
VE-NUS
GUY TRAP
WITH PHEROMONES
1069

TITIVATORS

TIVATORS
E DOZEN FLEXI-PACKS

re-mortgage the house to see it again?" In a word, no. Someone from Samuel French, the famous theatre publishers, attended a performance and they asked whether they could publish it. I think you can probably guess the answer. ***Sex Cells*** has now been performed in theatres all over the world, from New York to New Zealand. It's even been translated into Greek. This might not be the proper way to crash into show business, though apparently there is no 'proper' way. But once you've got in, you have to work just as hard to stay in. Anna was determined to prove that she was no one-hit wonder and knuckled down to write another. Her second production "***Curl Up and Die***" is a sell-out farce, which takes place in a run-down hairdressing salon. And guess what? That one's been published too. So now we're writing a musical about Edwardian footballers. A musical? I know, but it's going really well. Especially since I discovered that the word 'crotchet' has nothing to do with knitting, and a 'semi-quaver' isn't half of a cheese flavoured snack.

BASTARD

Lily on the
dear departed:

"I WANTED THEM TO OPEN HIM UP JUST TO SEE IF HE REALLY DID HAVE A BAD BACK"

# "I GOT CHUCKED SO I WENT ON A BENDER"

Tiffany on Romance:

COMI

ATHE

NEAR

IF YOU LIVE IN THE H

IG TO

ATRE

YOU!

IMERSMITH AREA

23
DNH 39122
TESCO
IVECO
BT65 CYO

OCEAN
RIVERSIDESTUDIOS
SEX CELLS.
A PLAY WITH A
FANCY POSTER
AS BIG AS THIS
MUST BE GOOD.
COMING TO A THEATRE NEAR YOU!
(If you live in the Hammersmith area)
SEX CELLS

UNLEASH THE POWER OF PUERILITY

# SEX CELLS.
# YET ANOTHER PLAY WITHOUT A SINGLE GOOD ROLE FOR A WOMAN.
# IT'S GOT FOUR.

Lily is brittle, Silvie is desperate, Janice is jaded and Tiffany is delightfully oblivious to everything. No wonder Mr Causeway is confused. Meet them all in 'Sex Cells' the bitterest, sweetest comedy by Anna Longaretti. Now available to perform. **www.samuelfrench.co.uk**

HOW NOT TO GET INTO SHOWBIZ!

SEX CELLS.
A PLAY FOR MOTHERS, WANT-TO-BE MOTHERS, AND ANYONE WHO'S EVER HAD A MOTHER.

In this bittersweet comedy, there's certainly no shortage of laughter and tears, just like motherhood really.
Now available to perform. **www.samuelfrench.co.uk**

Where are you going?
...to Ealing for a laugh!

ELENKA SVECOVA

BRYONY

JORDI CHINCHILL

RUTH HARRIS

MRS COTTERILL

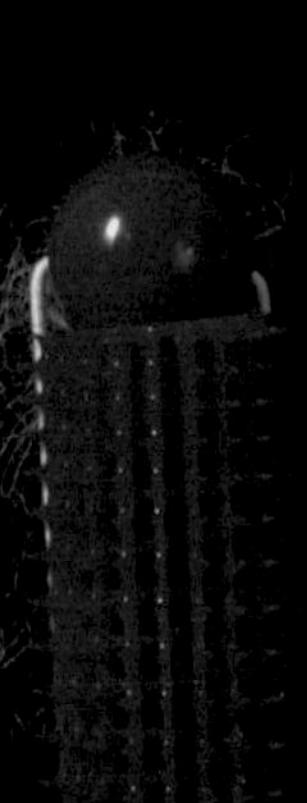

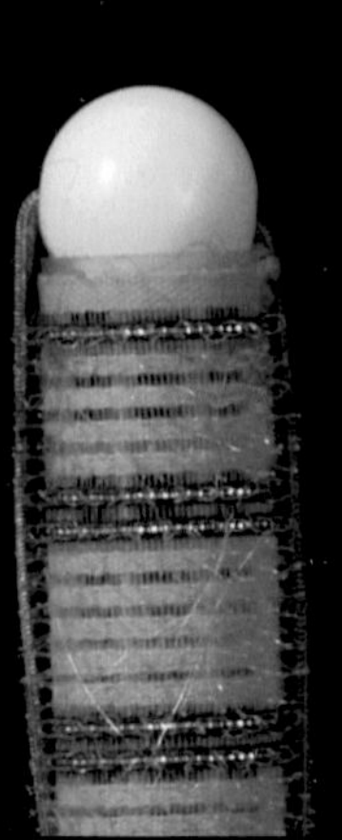

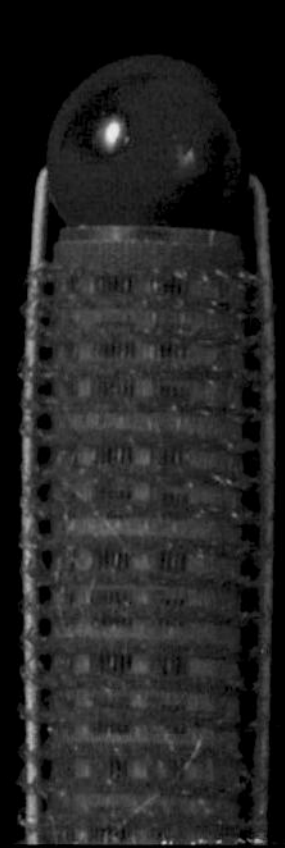

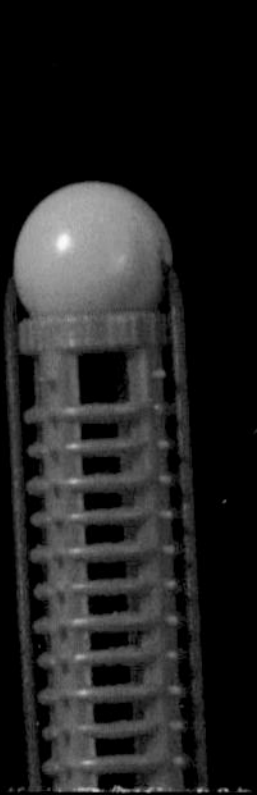

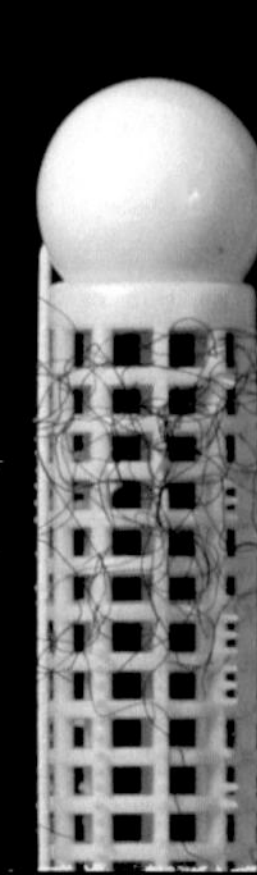

WOODPIGEON

DR.LEMON

GONKY BLATENT-SEVERS

MRS LUNDY

DOLLY C

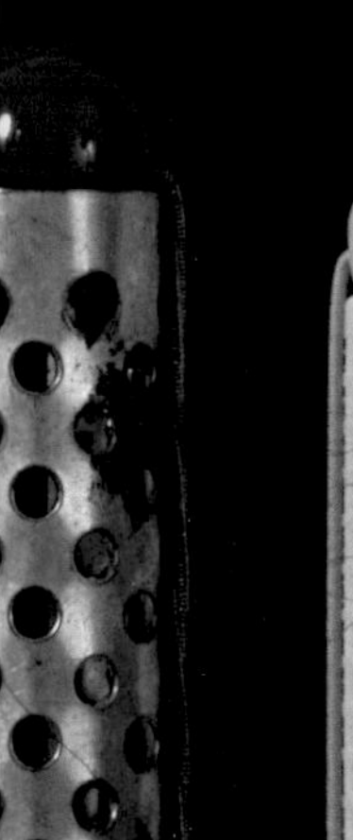

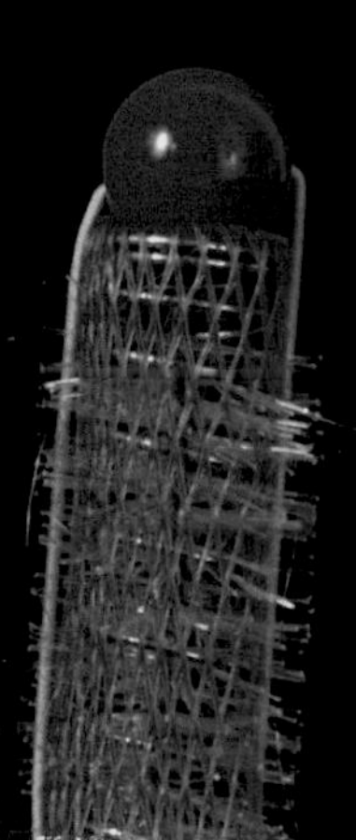

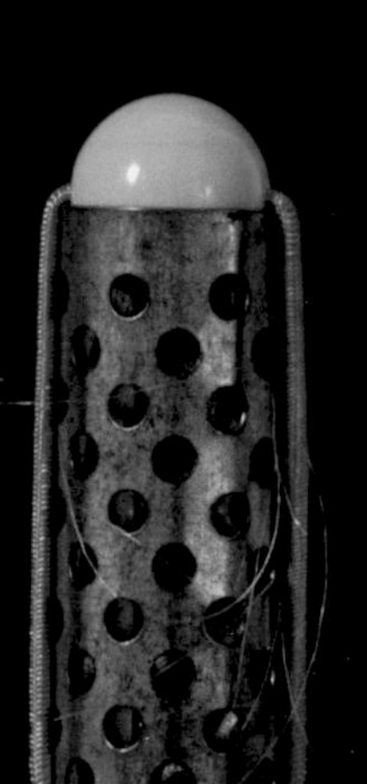

Fermé

# It's Blue-rinse Murder at t

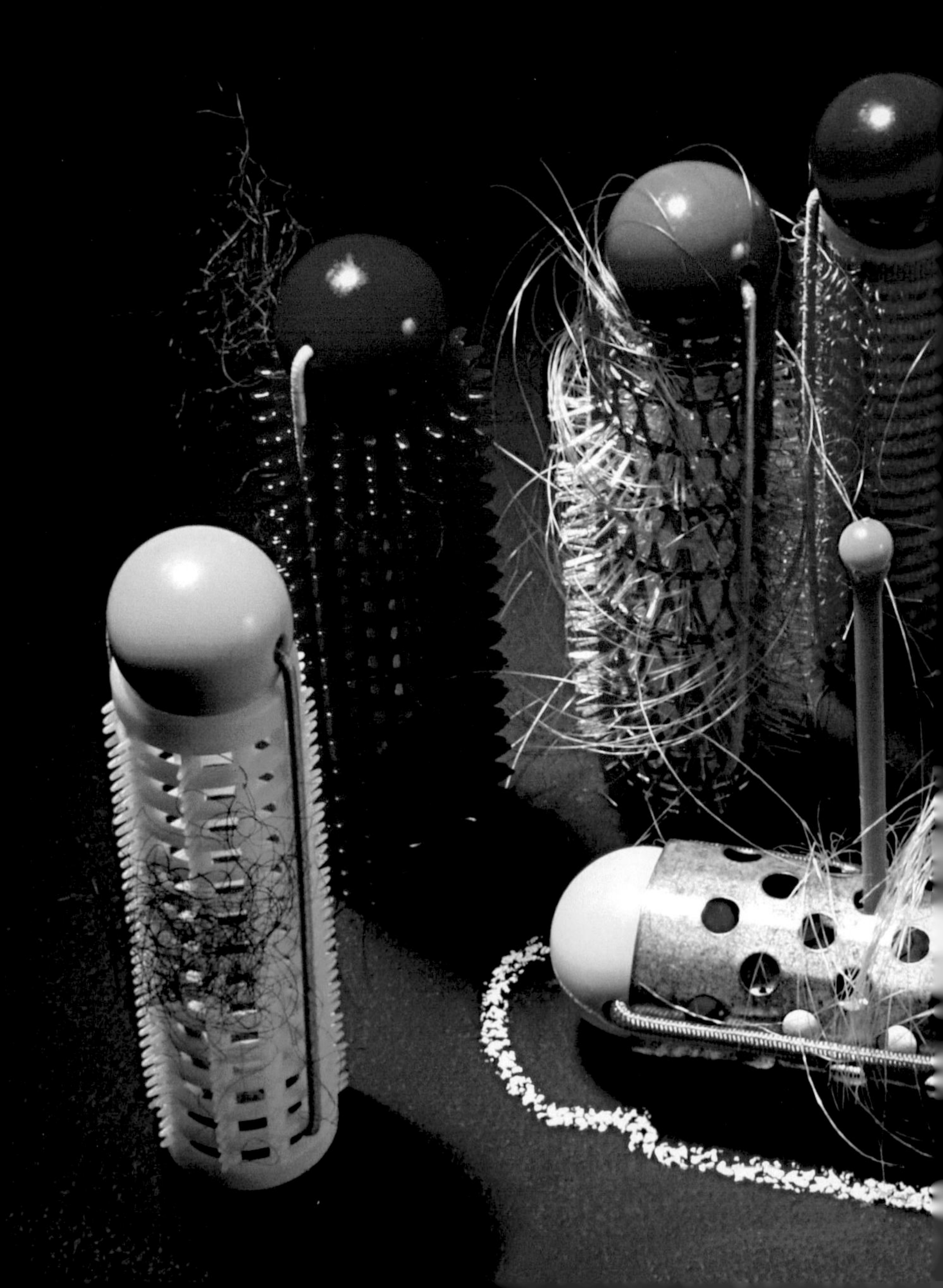

# Last chance Salon!

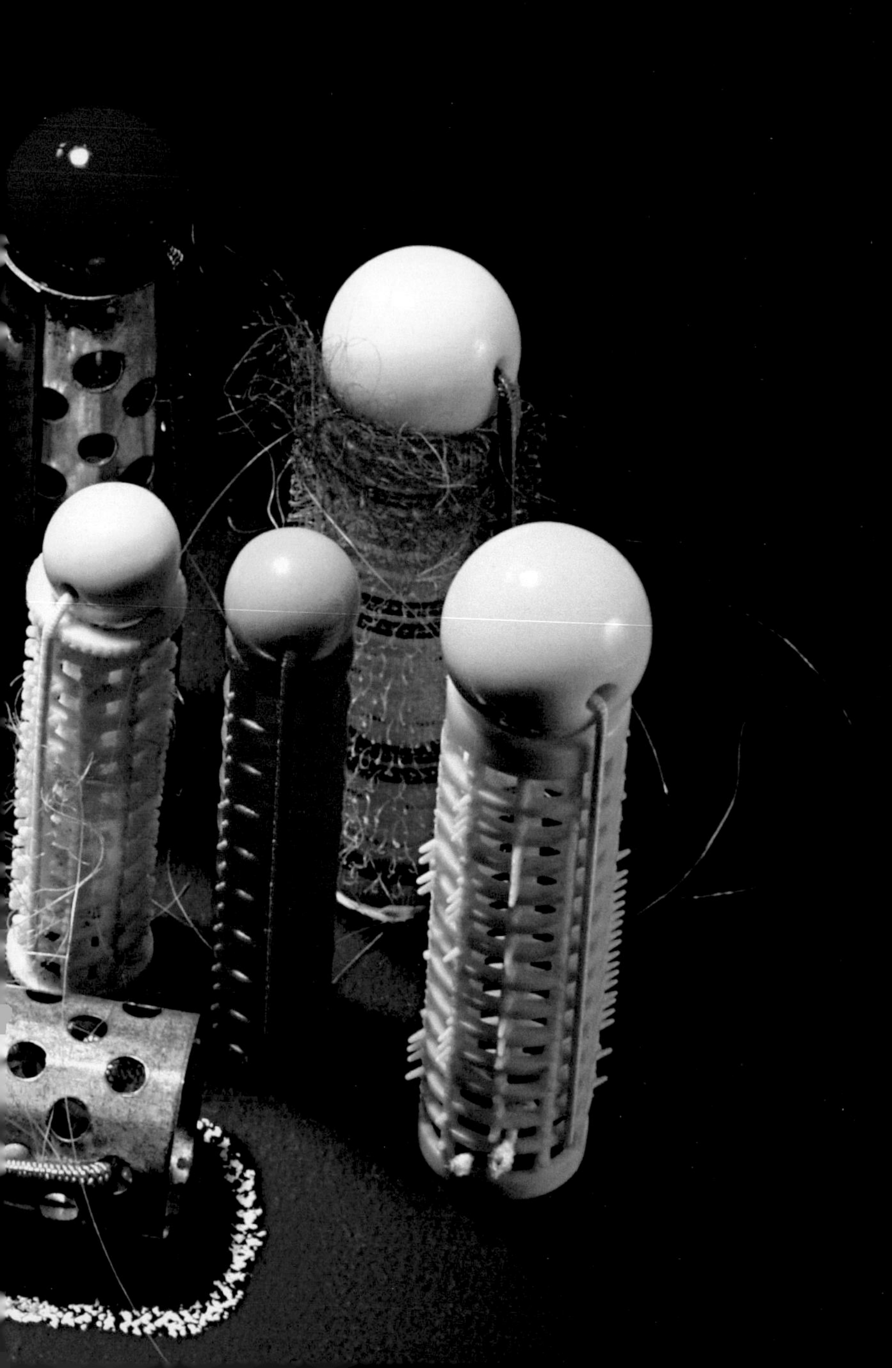

BEING
GETS

RESULTS!

It was a fit of pique. I'd said some rude words to an art director on a job but, quite mortified afterwards, I apologised profusely. Some people might argue that locking horns about creative work is justified and, rather than it being a fit of pique, you could see it as a fit of passion. Well, that's how I saw it. I was passionate about making the work as good as possible and I come from a time when creatives were expected to get stroppy to defend their work. But those days, it seems, are gone. Righteous anger is no longer an acceptable weapon in a creative's armoury. I'm not even sure 'weapon' is an acceptable word. And as for 'armoury'- let's not go there. Still, that didn't stop me feeling guilty and being a soppy - rather than stroppy - sod. I was still fretting about my little outburst more than a week later. So I aired the issue on social media to gauge the opinions of my mates in Adland. Almost immediately, Gordon Young, boss of The Drum Magazine, responded. He explained that, unwittingly, I'd timed my hissy

FUCK
OFF!

fit to perfection. Their next issue, he said, was called the 'Anger Issue' and he asked if I'd like to write a piece for it. Obviously I said yes, but exceeding my remit as usual, I suggested that I design the front cover too. With the help of ace COY! Photographer Joe Giacomet and our arty friends 'The Joy of Sets', (yes, it was me who came up with that name) we created a subtle little scenario with a disgruntled planner holding a meeting, complete with flip chart which bore the words FUCK and OFF! So that piece I'd written bemoaning the decline of stand-up rows in advertising agencies proved that clouds really do have silver linings. Even the one that had hung over me ever since my tantrum. Nowadays, I seldom have arguments and am rarely rude to anyone. However, I've never quite weaned myself off rudeness in its other incarnation. By which I mean filth. But like any weapon of mass-disruption, caution is advised. There has to be a good reason for its deployment. A fine example of strategically targeted filth was a poster I did for the lettering artist Alison Carmichael. Alison was lamenting the fact that, for the first time since she left college, her work had started to dry up. I said, "Leave it with me. I'll come up with some direct mail to help change that." I thought what about a beautiful realisation of the ugliest word in the English language. (The one that starts with a 'C' and rhymes with Berkshire Hunt). Under it would be the line 'Words look much nicer when they're hand lettered'. I was nervous about showing it to Alison. What if she hated it? And me for suggesting it? Fortunately, my fears were groundless. She absolutely LOVED it. She also loved the idea of screen-printing it on fancy paper. It worked a treat and Alison was suddenly getting commissions from all over the world. The limited edition C*NTs were also in great demand. I was told that someone even took one in to be framed. The framer in question took one look at it and, instead of being offended, said he'd frame it for free on one condition: Could he have a copy to give to his wife for their wedding anniversary? Even I was taken by surprise by the

Cunt
WORDS LOOK MUCH NICER WHEN THEY'RE HAND LETTERED
ALISON CARMICHAEL Lettering Artist phone/fax +44 (0)20 8789 3509 mobile +44 (0)775 398 6699 www.alisoncarmichael.com

**positive reaction. So with new found courage, we thought we'd take a punt and enter 'C*NT' for some awards. We held our breath and f*ck me, it only went and won a few. Emboldened by this, we entered it for the prestigious Design Week awards. It was shortlisted, so off we went to their swanky do at the Grosvenor House. With a title like that, we obviously didn't expect it to win. In fact, I thought we might get booed. So to make the most of the occasion, I had a ginormous pink cake made with C*NT iced on it for the COY! table. To our shock and delight, it won again. The best bit was the rather snooty compère having to announce "And the winner is C*NT!" Though some people might have thought she was referring to the bald bloke on his way up to the podium. Alison was then so busy that we never got round to completing the campaign. The next one up was meant to be 'TURD' (Words are more polished when they're hand lettered) to be followed by 'WANK' (It's better when done by hand). On another occasion, I was**

shots
Mark
Denton
ON LIFE LESSONS
& THE LACK OF
GOLDEN EGGS
150th Special
THE 150 MOST CREATIVE
PEOPLE, COMPANIES & WORK
Cannes Focus
AMIR KASSAEI, JAIME ROBINSON &
THIS YEAR'S CROISETTE CONTENDERS
Andreas Nilsson
A DIRECTOR WHO GETS
UNDER YOUR SKIN

**invited to write an article for SHOTS Magazine. My theme was the decline of creatives' power within agencies. In short, how they were once the geese who laid the golden eggs but were now treated more like battery hens. If you wrote a piece for SHOTS, you could provide an accompanying image. And if they liked it, they'd consider it for the front cover. So I sat down to think of a winning image. I sat there and strained and strained and finally I thought, "Yes!" I told Anna and she said "No! Have you taken leave of your senses?" I said, "You're right. I can't do that". So obviously, I did it. The image was me, squatting bare-arsed over a golden egg. I thought it'd be a relatively easy shoot. Once it was lit, I'd quickly drop my pants assume the position and snap, snap; flash, flash, pull pants back up. Job done. But no, it wasn't quite as simple as that. Sean, the photographer, insisted on me holding that position for ages while a gold reflector was positioned where the egg would be. So I was squatting interminably over a mirror, while a studio full**

of people looked on. But it was well worth the embarrassment because SHOTS chose it for their souvenir 'Cannes' issue front cover. Art, cakes, front covers, there's no limit to where a penchant for the very rude can take you, including film. Sean Doyle is one of the funniest copywriters I know and he draws hilarious cartoons too. He'd drawn one about a porn star who got over-excited while filling his car up with petrol. Once I'd seen it, I felt a strange compulsion to fly to Spain with a film crew and bring it to life. As usual, there was no plan, I didn't know what I was going to do with the film, I only knew I absolutely had to shoot it. I cast a fantastic actor called - I swear I'm not making this up - Peter Cocks to play our hero. Anna miraculously transformed him into a 1970s porn star with wig, fake eyebrows, 'tache and chest hair. It was a great laugh and once it had been skilfully cut together by editor Joel Miller to a perfect soundtrack written by Vince Pope, I knew we had something special. We held a little screening in a viewing theatre in Soho and that

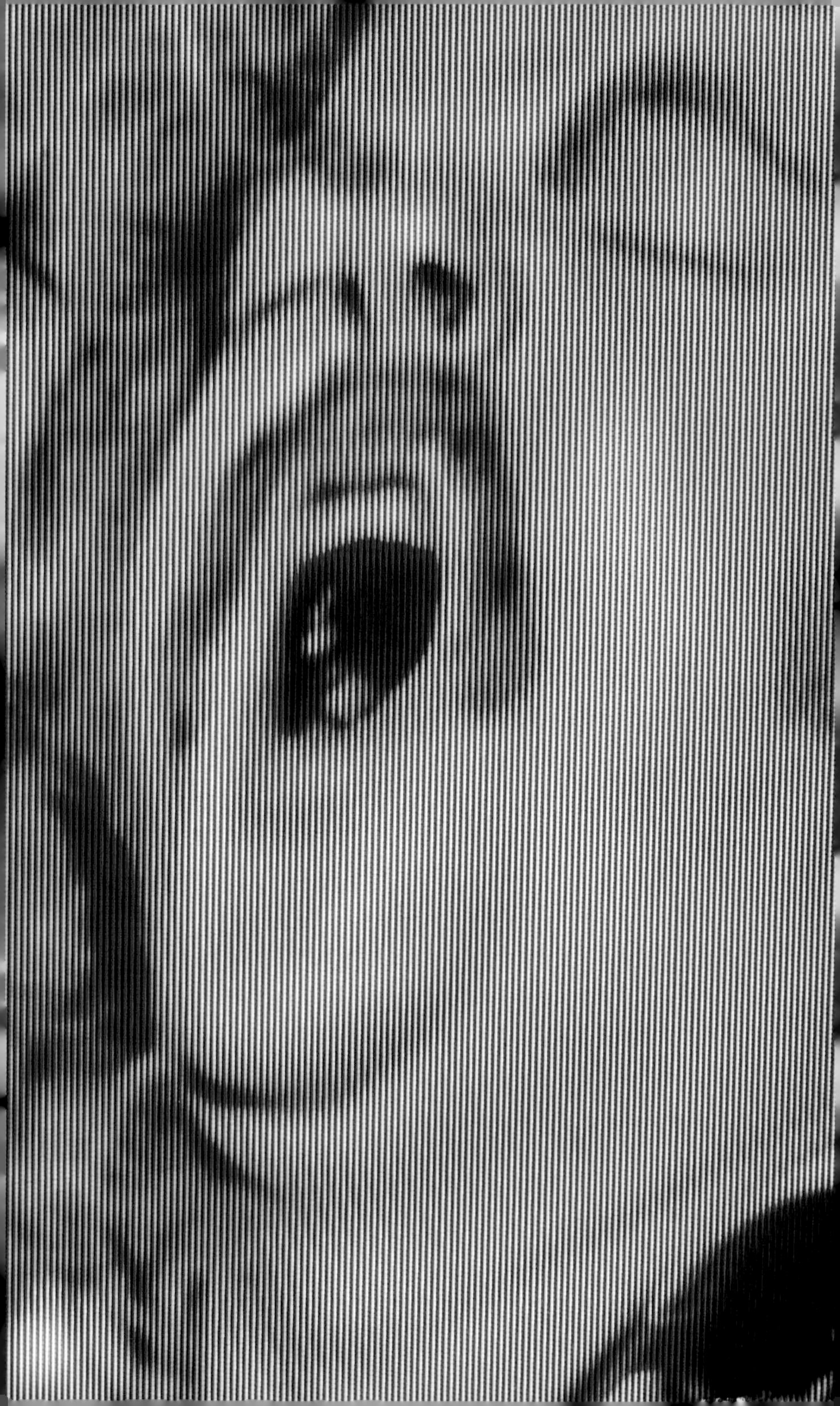

**was the end of that. Except it wasn't. As you probably now realise, it never is. Channel 4 saw it, bought the rights and pretty soon my dad was boasting to his neighbours about his son having a film on the telly. Oh, all right then - one more rude story. Last one, mind. I needed a press ad to announce the opening of COY! The ad in question was originally supposed to be a sponsorship ad for the Creative Circle Annual. I'd invited top creative teams to submit ideas for it and the one sent in by Carl Broadhurst and Peter Reid was an absolute corker. It was basically the COY! logo tattooed onto a naked bum and artfully shot by the brilliant James Day. I was so delighted with it that I took out a double-page spread in Campaign to show it off. I knew I'd done the right thing when I saw a visitor to our office leafing through a copy in reception. She physically recoiled when she got to the COY! ad. She shut the mag quickly but clearly having braced herself, went back to the page and started laughing. See? Being rude really does get results.**

TARHAH!

RUMBLE!

SNORT!

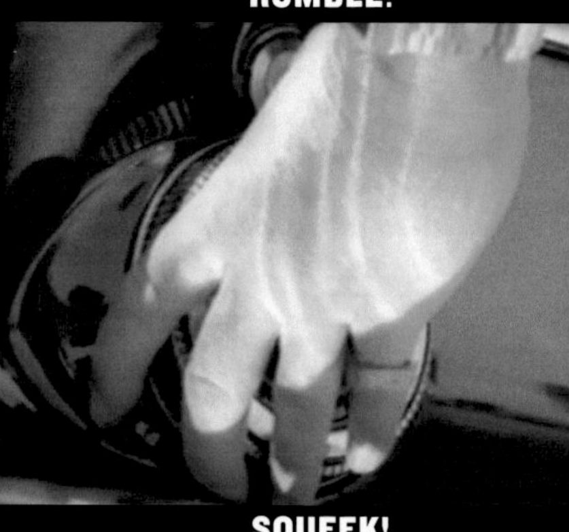

SQUEEK!

CLANG! CLANG!

RATTLE!

GUSHH!

SPLASH!

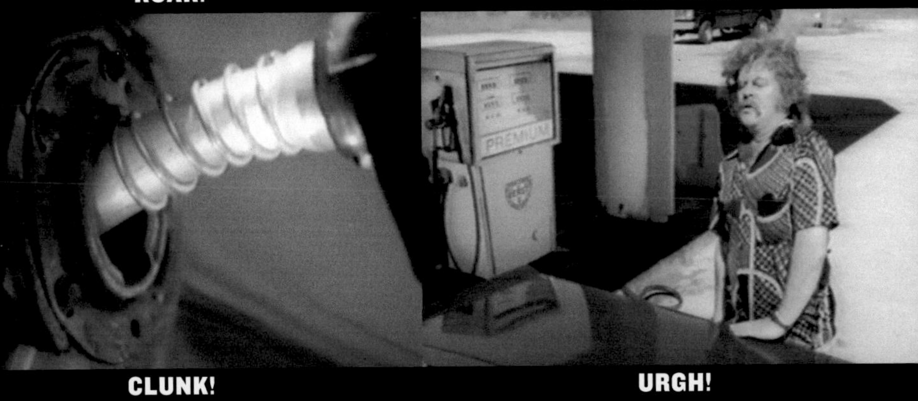


SPURT!

AAAARRRGH!

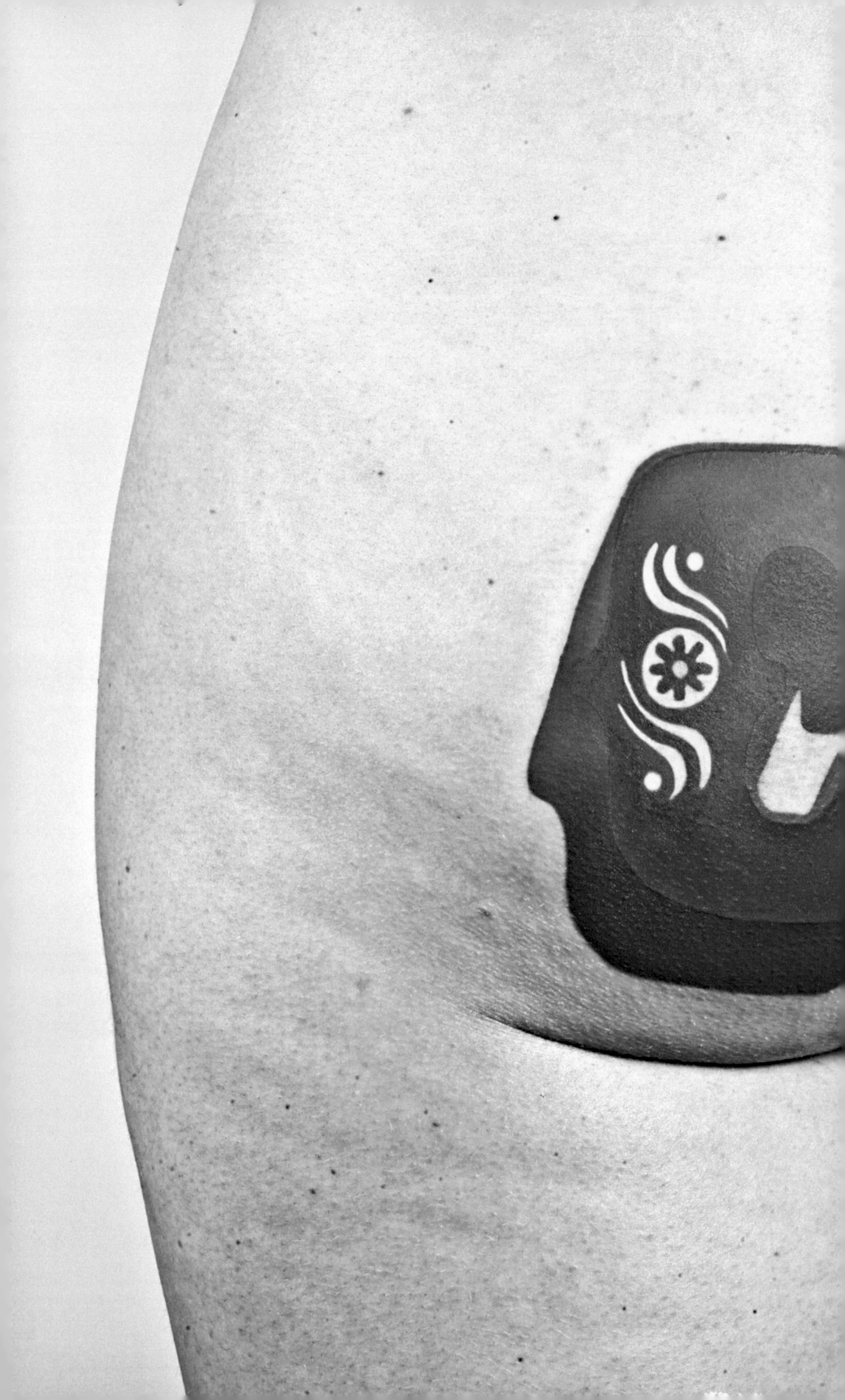

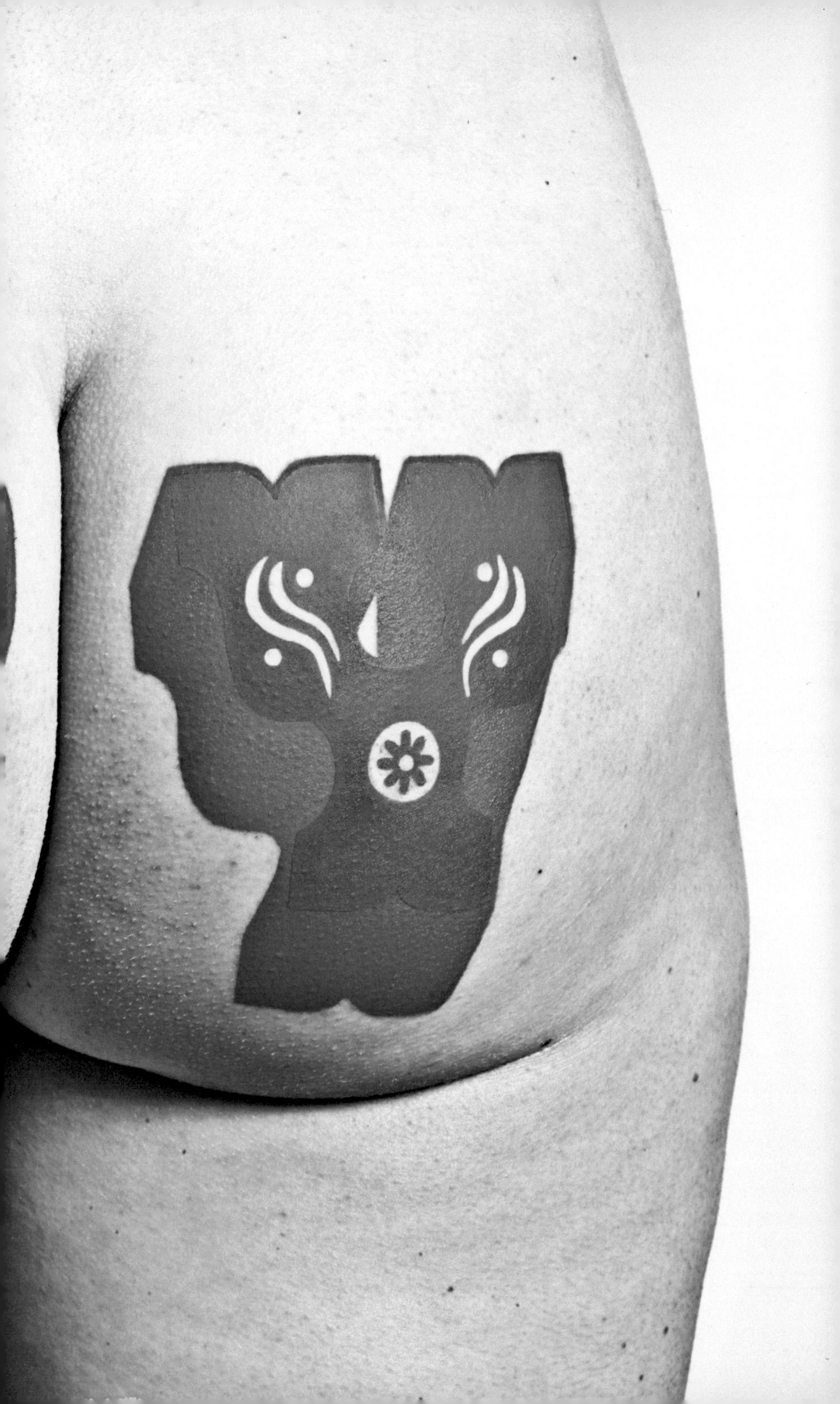

# ...Just in case it all gets a b

o much **LOOK AT THIS!**

JUD
BY ITS
CO

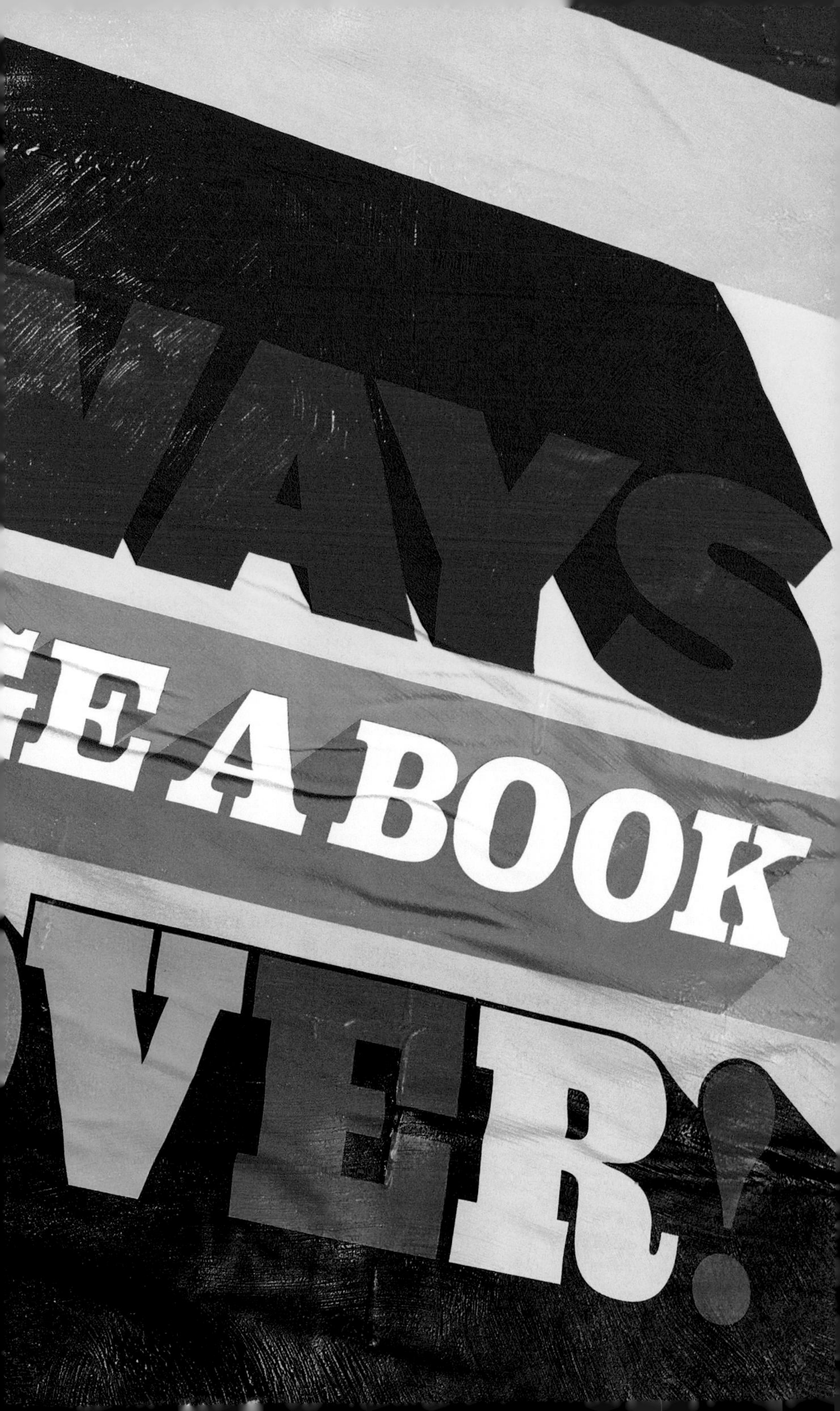

AYS
E A BOOK
VER!

**'Never judge a book by its cover'. Probably the daftest advice to give to anyone. Far wiser to say "Always judge a book by its cover". In Stone Age times, before even I was born, your life could depend on making a quick judgment about the man or beast in front of you. The whole business of advertising and design was built on creating a favourable first impression. And if books weren't judged by their covers, I doubt you'd be reading this one. When I was in possession of a full head of hair and my first credit card, shop assistants always judged what was in front of them. If I was scruffily attired, a call would usually be made to the credit card company for 'security reasons'. However, when I was wearing a suit, that call was never deemed necessary. Fortunately a good whistle has long been my apparel of choice, I got the bespoke bug at the tender age of thirteen: that's when my dad proudly took me to be fitted for my first made-to-measure suit. His mood soon changed though when he found out what kind of suit I'd specified. In 1969, you see, 'skinhead' was**

TEST: WARDROBE
JOB: 'ART-MART' TO
NOTES: GHETTO GOL
DATE: 24.11.

DEN TON

very much the style of the day. And with its tight cut and narrow lapels, my new petrol blue 'Tonik' suit embodied that style perfectly. From that moment on, I decided that - by hook or by crook - whatever I wore would be hand-made (or at least hand-altered) to my personal specifications. Even as an impoverished student, I adapted old knitting patterns to my own designs and begged my Mum, Gran and Auntie Elsie into knitting them up for me. They didn't need much persuading because they LOVED knitting and that's how I first discovered how to corral creative people to a cause. Simply offer them the chance to do what they love. So that I could do my bit to help, I signed up for evening classes in dressmaking and tailoring which enabled me to alter any suits that I'd bought from charity shops. To be honest, I wasn't great with a needle and thread. So as soon as I was earning a half-decent salary, I was giving most of it to people who made clothes for a living. From hand-made suits, I progressed to hand-made shirts, shoes, hats and tracksuits, lots of tracksuits. And the process is the same one I adopt for all creative endeavours: draw a picture, colour it in, then get a talented person to make it a reality. A lot of gifted people have helped me hang individually designed, tailor-made garments in my wardrobe, especially my tremendous tailor of twenty years, Spyros Christodoulou. He coincidentally retired around the same time as I succumbed to the lure of an elasticated waistband. Fortunately, being a commercials director meant that I got to meet some terrific costume designers that have helped to create most of my leisurewear. But I really must single out Spencer Horne for special recognition. Spencer is responsible for all of those tracksuits I mentioned and for a little invention of mine, jeans made out of tweed (or Tweans, as we call them). Invariably they're in some kind of check, as is much of my favourite apparel, so here's a top tip: If you're ever worried about two checks clashing, just add a third, fourth, or even fifth check to the mix. People will say it looks amazing and assume this wild checkfest

ARDROBE
MART TOUR
HIS 'N' HERS
DATE: 24.11.17

TEST: WARDROBE
JOB: 'ART-MART' TOUR
NOTES: GHETTO GOLFER
DATE: 24·11·17

TON

has been carefully worked out, even if it hasn't. Correction: especially if it hasn't. I've always been fascinated by tailors. A couple of years ago, I was contacted by a very talented young woman called Rachel Singer. We'd met before when she was pursuing a career in graphic design. But she'd changed tack and was now following her true vocation: she'd embarked upon an apprenticeship with Maurice Sedwell, one of the most esteemed tailors in Savile Row. Which, of course, means one of the most esteemed tailors in the world. I really admired her for that. "Would I", Rachel enquired, "be up for commissioning her first piece of bespoke tailoring?" "You bet!" I said, and thought it only fair to make the commission a bit of a challenge. So, at my behest, the finished suit had hundreds of pearl buttons stitched into the waistcoat. Rachel did such a wonderful job that I asked her to make me a range of 'magic' trousers to complement the hats I'd had specially conjured up by celebrated milliner Jane Smith (the lady behind Laurel and Hardy's bowlers for the film Stan & Ollie). Anyway, it's all very well having a bulging wardrobe full of custom-made clobber but where it really pays dividends is when you walk around town in it. It's funny how many people want to say hello to you when you're sporting a snazzy pair of trousers. These conversations have led to me being asked by the BBC to talk about my passion for clothes and to be featured in countless fancy fashion magazines like Arena and ID. Mind you, it's best not to let the added attention you get from dapper-dressing go to your head. I remember one time, dressed in my new black and white pinstriped suit, striding down Wardour Street in Soho. I was aware of heads turning and smiles coming my way as I confidently twirled my umbrella. The sun was shining, I felt good, I knew I looked smart; no wonder I was getting more than my fair share of attention. It was only when I got to the end of the street that I noticed that my flies were wide open and my shirt was protruding comically from the gaping hole.

CIRCLE
HEAD

FOR
DRUFF
BLINK
with added BLAH!
UP WITH NOSEY
Styling
LARD
EXTRA FIRM HOLD
EVIL
THERAPY

SPROTE
THE CREATIVE CIRCLE 2008
Styling
LARD
EXTRA FIRM HOLD
thoughts from the Head of advertising
RUGGED

WHY WHISPER

WHEN YOU C

SHOU

**Advertising is about raising awareness and the simplest way to raise awareness is to raise your voice. Make yourself heard, get yourself seen. What's the point of doing anything good if no one knows about it? Yet one thing has always baffled me: How come ad agencies are so good at advertising other people's products but so bad at promoting themselves? Whenever I do anything that I think is worth shouting about, I make sure that shouting is exactly what I do. Obviously I splash it all over social media, but I also create some good old-fashioned print work in the style of a newsvendor's 'headline' poster. On one side I plaster a grabby headline and on the other side an equally grabby picture. And if I feel like giving the poster a bit of extra heft, I'll wrap it round a custom-made 'COY!' rubber brick. With or without the brick, the posters always go down well. So well, in fact, that a lot of people put them up on their walls where they get seen by even more people. Now you don't get that with an email. I've made some**

95%
INSECTS
ARE

*fig* A.

*fig* B.

*fig* C.

**pretty preposterous pronouncements on those posters over the years. From profound pearls of wisdom like '*95% of Insects are Shit*', life's challenging existential questions like '*Juan Nille or Tu Wun?*' and plain old lies like boasting about COY!'s first ever £1 trillion advertising campaign. But the most popular poster so far was the one for the 'Edible Anus Company' (Yes. *Edible Anus* - you did read that correctly). After the initial mail-out, I sold bundles of them (Yes, *sold* - you read that correctly too). The poster for the Edible Anuses (Don't panic. They're a delectable brand of chocolates but in the shape of a you-know-what), featured a big photograph of a standard motorway sign. However, the destinations it displayed had rather unusual names like 'Milk' and 'Lemonade'. There was even a little slip road which led round the corner to the local chocolate factory. Anyway, here's a small selection. So, as I said - I mean as I *shouted* '*READ ALL ABOUT IT!* READ ALL ABOUT IT! READ ALL ABOUT IT! *READ ALL ABOUT IT!!***

D&AD
GOOD

D&AD 12
DENTON

ALL ABOUT IT! READ ALL ABOUT I

EAD ALL ABOUT IT! READ ALL ABO

RAC

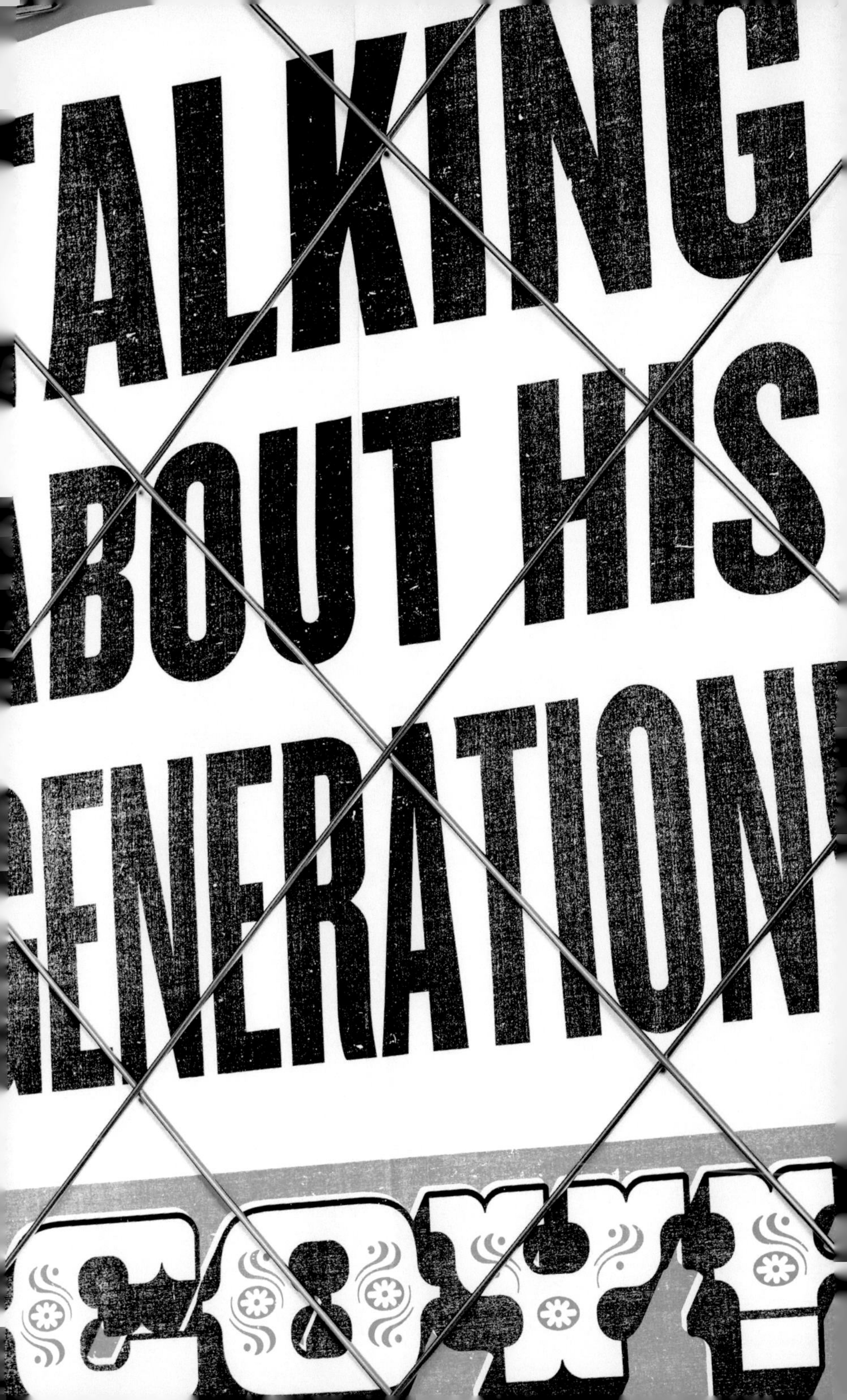
ALKING
BOUT HIS
ENERATION

OY!
RUBBISH
SURFER
CAPTURED!
COY!
COMMUNICATIONS

COY LAUNCH
TRILLION

POSTER
CAMPAIGN!

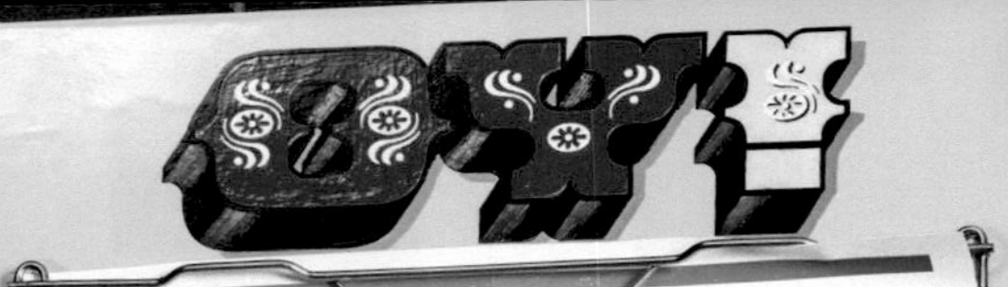

COPY!
IN-DEPTH PROBE
EXCITING NEW OPENING IN CHOCOLATE CATEGORY!
COPY!
COMMUNICATIONS
The Milky Bums are on Me
edibleanus.com

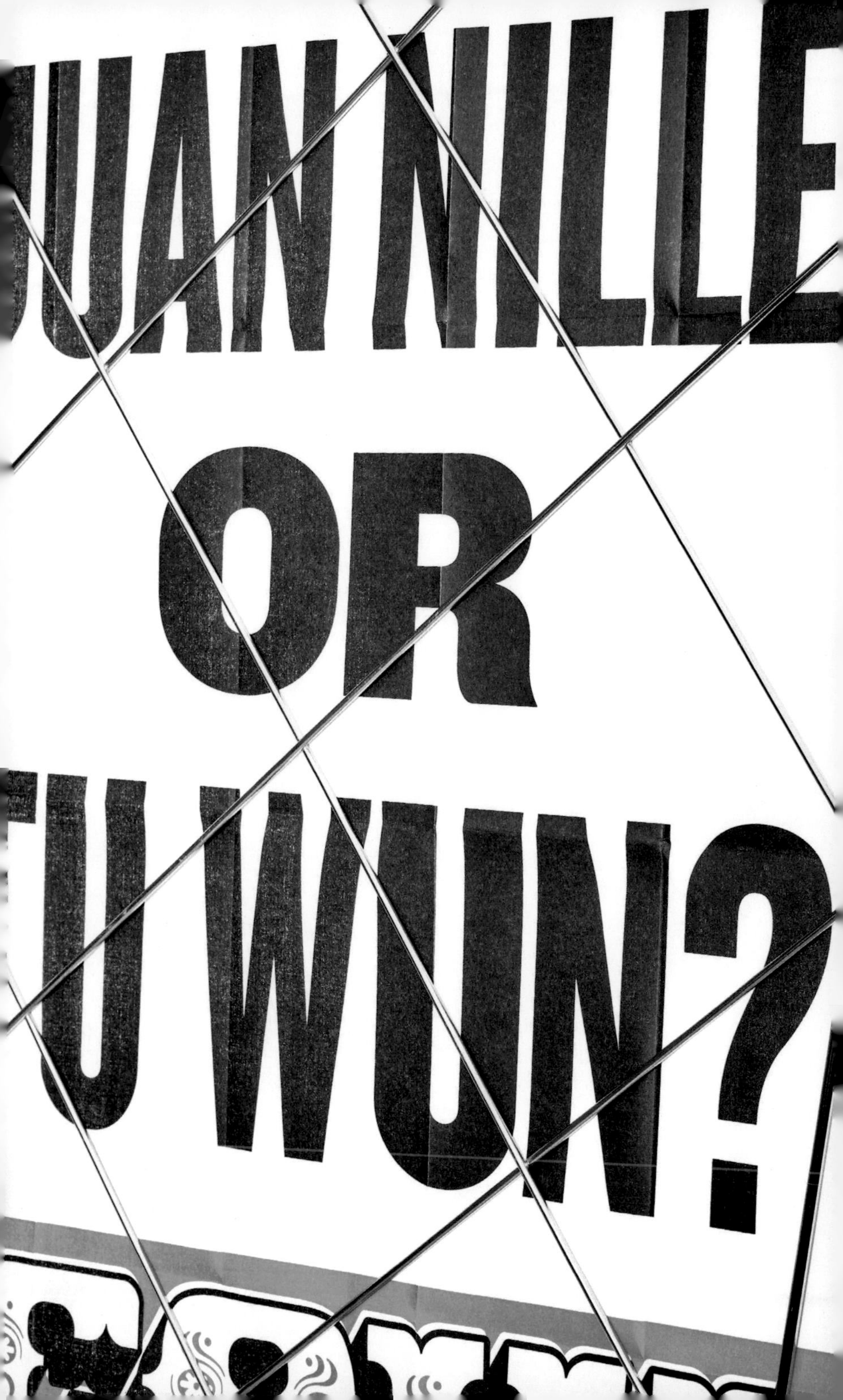
UAN MILLE
OR
U WUN?

JUAN NILLE
LEFT-OUTSIDE
FAKE MADRID

DIRTY
TOOLS
-THING
OF PAST!
COXY
COMMUNICATIONS
FILTHY
HOES

MEET
MODEST
THE SHY
& RETIRIN
COY CUT

WHICH IS BREW?

COMMUNICATIONS

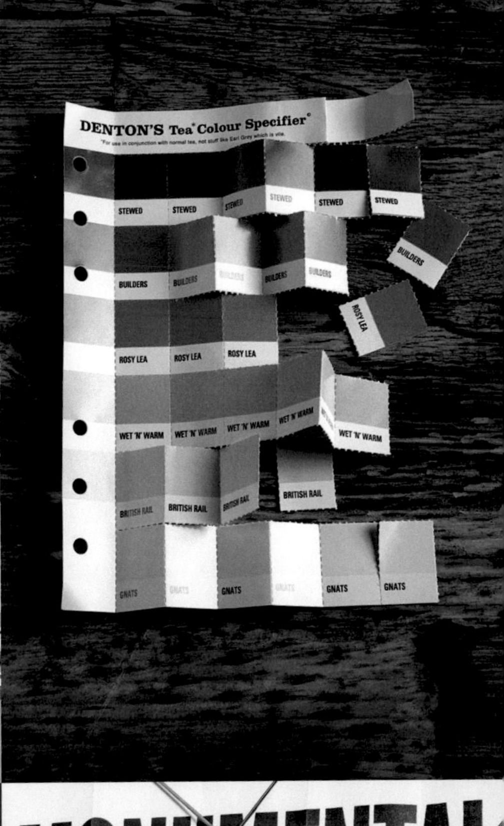


MONUMENTAL ERECTION UNVEILED!

…INE NEEDED A PHOTOGRAPHIC IMAGE FOR THEIR SPECIAL 'HEROES' ISSUE, SO WE GAVE THEM A MONUMENTAL ONE OF OUR LEADER … GIVEN FOR
…A PROPER BRONZE STATUE BUT IN REALITY IT WAS A CLEVER BIT OF MAKE-UP BY …

# LADY FROM
# LLANFAIRPWLL
# GWYNGYLLGO
# ERYCHWYRND
# OBWLLLLANT
# SILIOGOGOGOC
# LOVES LETTERS

(JUST AS WELL REALLY)

BBBB
Bernheardt

CHANGE OF
DIRECTION
FOR NEW
EDIBLE ANUS
CAMPAIGN!

COMMUNICATIONS

Milk
Milk
Chocolate
Lemonade
40

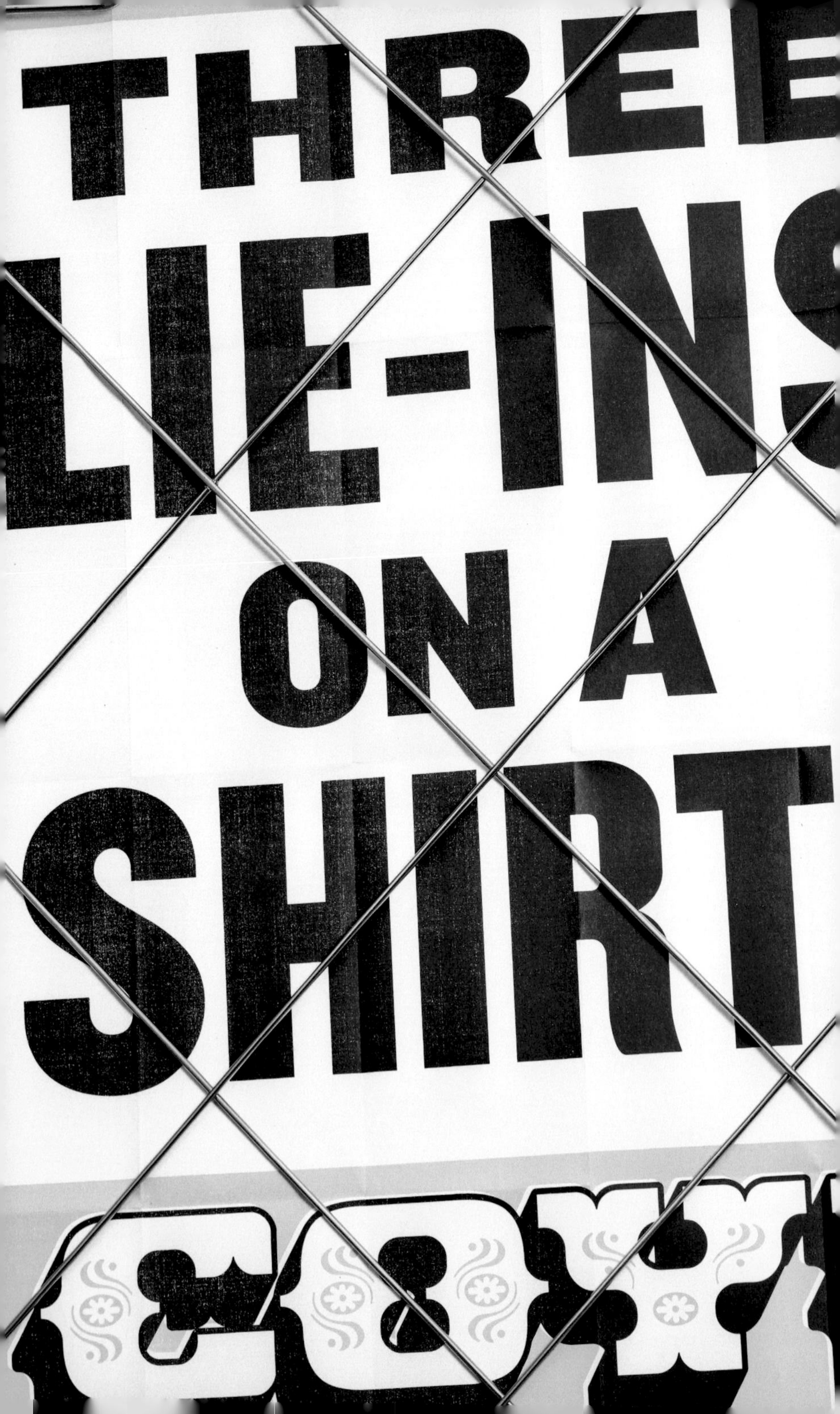
THREE
LIE-INS
ON A
SHIRT

NOTVERY ATHLETIC

ALLIANCE ACP
AWY

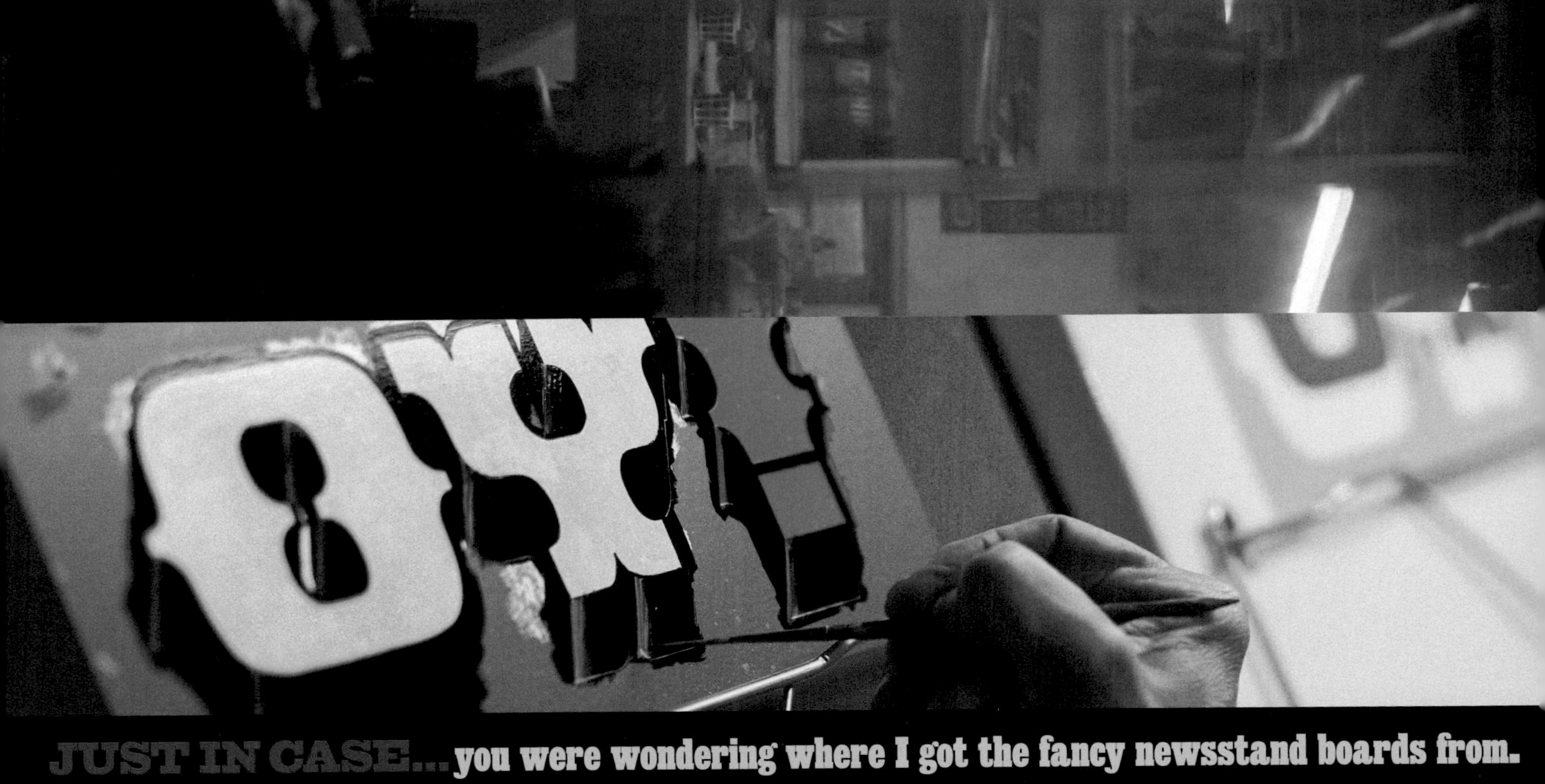

**JUST IN CASE...** you were wondering where I got the fancy newsstand boards from. I had them made, sprayed, gold chromed, gilded and hand lettered.... it seemed silly not to.

MORE
by MIS

agic
AKE!

**Remember that I began this book by talking about how things seem to happen by magic when you apply the Power of Puerility? Well this is definitely the final - and might just be the finest-example of how those magical happenstances can occur. Now I have a little confession to make: I love business cards. Yes, I know that they're a bit old-fashioned but I think that's why I like them. I like designing them, collecting them, receiving them and handing them out. They're still such a friendly and effective way of introducing yourself and staying remembered. Especially if you hand them out at events where, shall we say, drink has been taken. Like any piece of communication, the more creative a business card, the less likely it is to be thrown away or forgotten. I've got a very fine selection, each featuring portraits of yours truly in one of a whole host of ridiculous guises. Each one has been painstakingly 'produced' with different printing processes including varnishing, foiling and laminating. So they actually *feel* even**

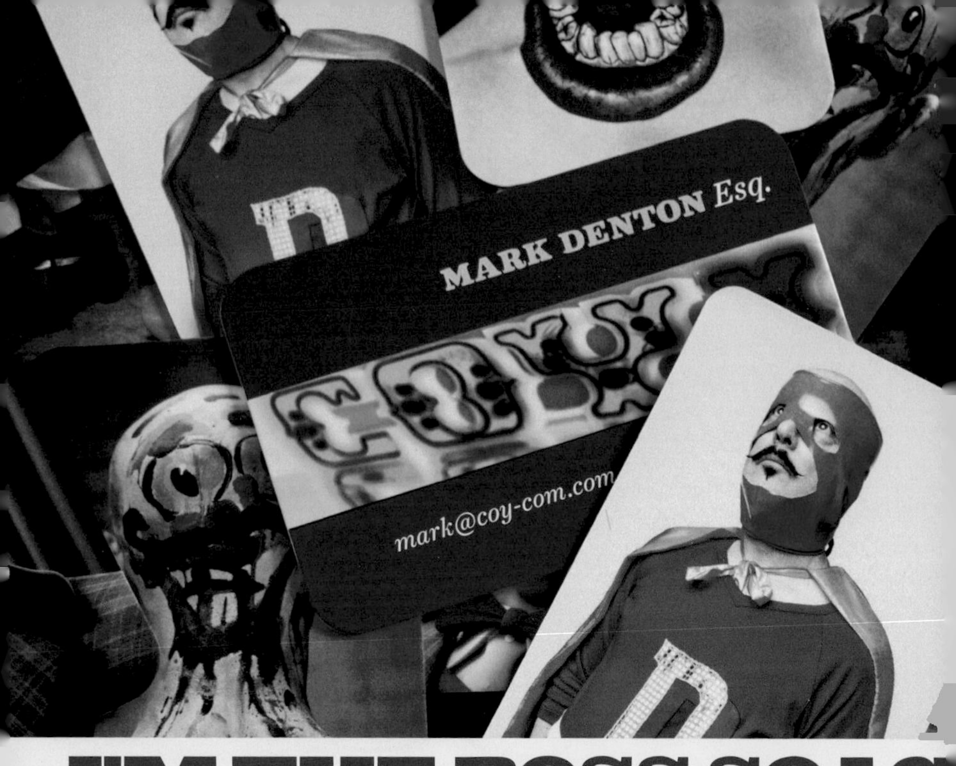


# I'M THE BOSS SO I G

# THE MOST CARDS!

**better than they look. As a result, everyone at COY! has a business card with at least one splendiferous picture on it. Take my enthusiastic producer Juan Coello Hollebecq. It wouldn't take Inspector Morse to work out that he doesn't come from Catford. No, Juan is from Venezuela and even I know that's somewhere in South America. I also know that South Americans often seem to have a penchant for dictators, so naturally I turned Juan into a dictator for his business card. The budget didn't quite stretch to a proper military uniform, replete with medals, so we improvised one with old cardboard boxes, beer-cans and bottle tops. And then there's my delightful, diminutive designer Kate Henderson. Kate's Chinese, from a little town just west of Beijing called Croydon. Kate likes cats (a lot) so I thought I could stick some ears and whiskers on her, paint her gold and she could pose as one of those lucky cats with the waving paw. She was totally up for it which got me thinking: If she's happy to be painted,**

**then why not paint her blue like that very famous kitsch 'Chinese Girl' print that hung in everyone's living rooms in the 60s. With the help of my trusted and talented team; Saskia on blue paint and paintbrush, Anna (the Missus) on hair, Emily and Sabina on wardrobe and photographer Joe Giacomet behind the camera, Kate looked sensational. So sensational that it seemed silly to just take one picture, pack up and go home. So alongside our version of the iconic 'Chinese Girl' portrait, I stuck a fag in her mouth and asked her to give us a bit of Croydon 'attitude'. Then came versions of her dressed as a Commie, stuffing her face with doughnuts, blowing bubble gum and doing a bit of DIY. They turned out so well that I couldn't resist posting them out on social media (as one does) and was delighted when they got hundreds of "likes". While I was on Facebook I noticed that my good friend Dave Buonaguidi was having an exhibition of his screen prints at 'Jealous', a fashionable East End gallery, so I thought I'd**

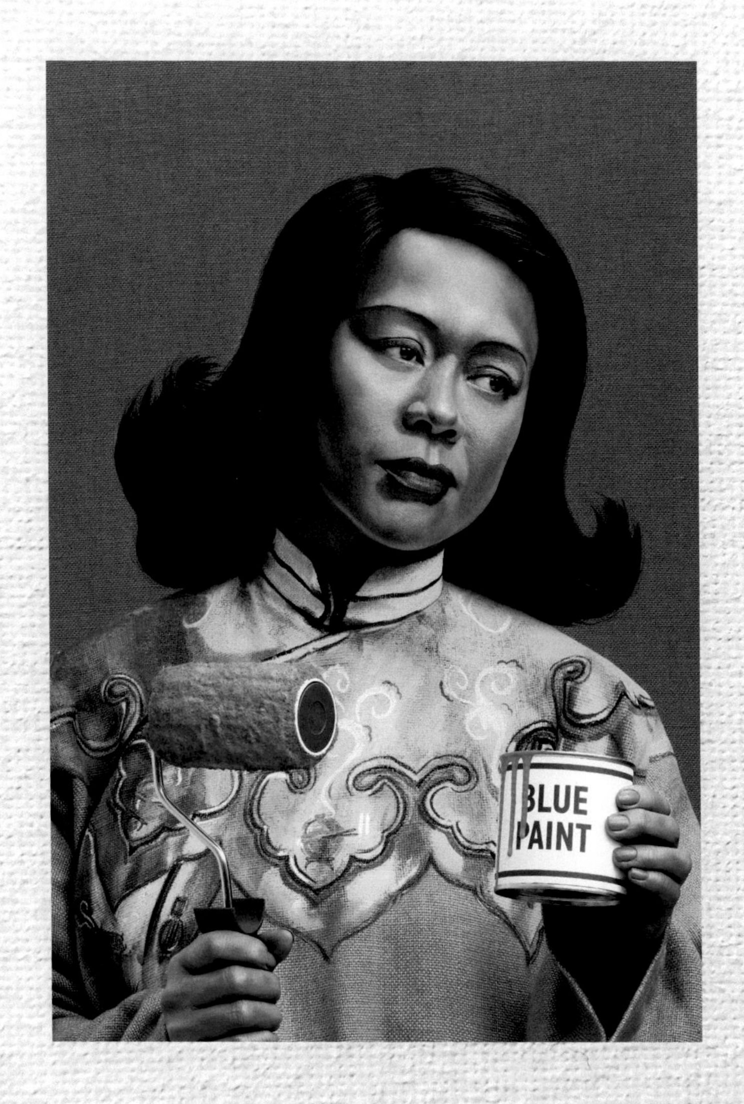
BLUE
PAINT

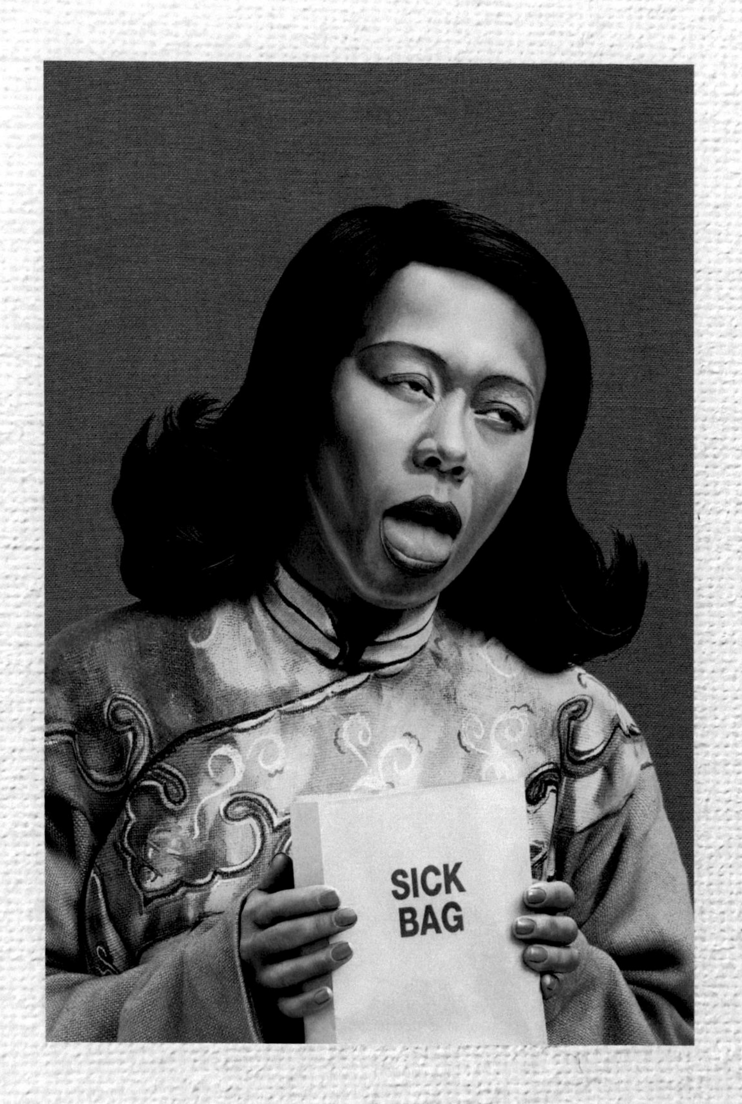
SICK
BAG

QUOTATIONS FROM
CHAIRMAN
MAO TSETUNG

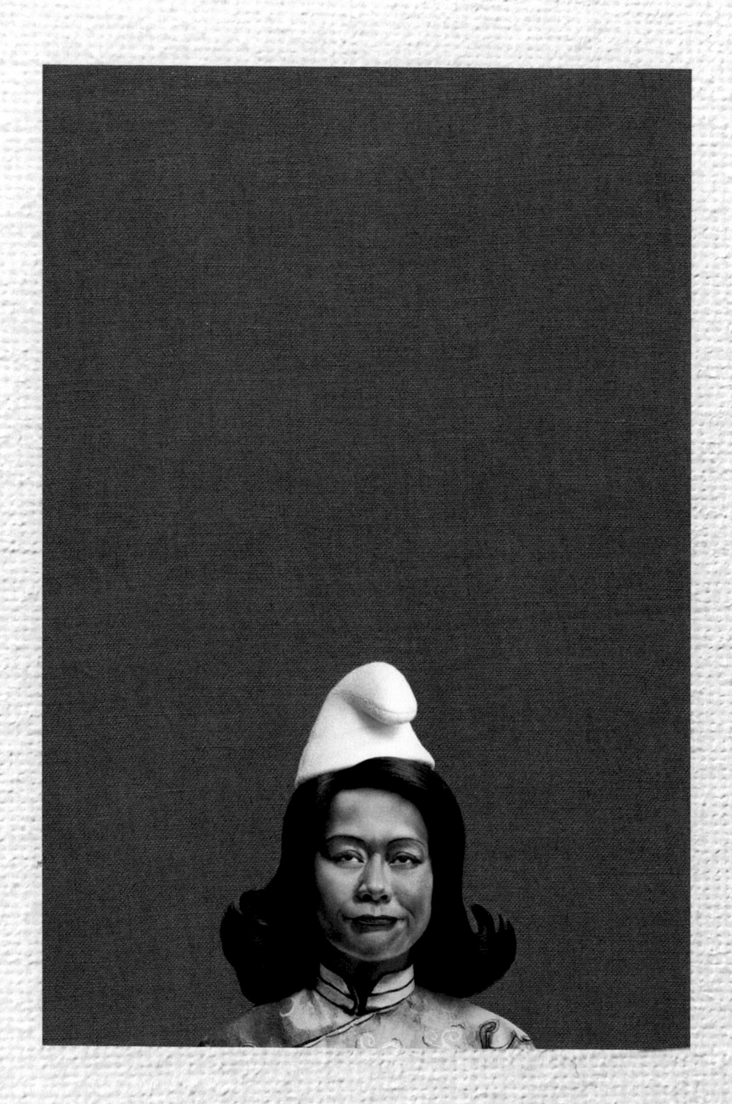

**pop down and buy a print. When I got there I started chatting (I like a chat) to a bloke who turned out to be the gallery owner, Dario. I proudly showed him the pictures that we'd just shot of Kate and, before you know it, I had the offer of a two week exhibition. Of course I was excited about the prospect of putting on my my own show but, instead of just hanging some pictures on a gallery wall, what about transforming the whole place into a supermarket, selling high-end art at knock-down prices? Yep, that felt even more exciting. I did a quick scribble and gave it to my talented friends Jess and Alex AKA 'The Joy of Sets' and they concocted a truly super supermarket. The art comprised loads of images from my back catalogue with three 'Chinese Girl from Croydon' pictures taking pride of place in big, gold frames. I employed a signwriter, courtesy of 'Better Letters', to paint the front window. And a bunch of beautiful supermarket signs hand-lettered by Mike Meyer. This was my first 'proper'**

ONE TIME OFFER!
POPPED Cherries
39
Dresse
LOOSE
Easter

ART
PITH OFF
Peeled Grapefruit SEGMENTS 59p
Humongous Melons
LOOSE £2.00
Heffer LUMPS
Big!
GIANT NUT SACK
PER SACK
Special
BOILED BUNNIES
IN A CAN
99p
A CLUMP
JAM
55p
EVIL
Heffer LUMPS
BOILED BUNNY
The Graphic Works of
ART MART!
BLUE PAINT
JEALOUS OFFERS

art
ME OFFER!
POPPED
Cherries
Easter Spe
BOILE
RACK
OF LAMB £2.50
HAM
FISTS
ONLY
2.50
Each!
PON
Dresse
MUT
Very Limited Offe
One way
RK DENTON Esq.
EVIL

**exhibition and, I thought, it may well be my last so I wanted to make an impact. I even got some 'Green Lady' beer specially brewed with an image of Kate puking into a sick-bag on the label. It was a tremendous night and the following morning, Dario came clean. He said that he hadn't expected to sell a single piece of art but in fact, we'd sold a shedload. The pictures of Kate had proved particularly popular. And that, I thought, was that. But it wasn't. Of course it wasn't. A few months later, I got a very nice, very formal letter from the Royal Academy of Arts, informing me that two of my pictures had been accepted for their Summer Exhibition. Dario had only gone and entered both of Kate's portraits without telling me. My work in the Royal Academy! I mean, much as I love D&AD and Creative Circle, this was a totally different league. Naturally I went along to the show about a dozen times, not just because my pictures were in it, but also because it had been curated by Grayson Perry, one of my all time heroes.**

**A week or so later, BBC2 did a programme about the exhibition, presented by Kirsty Wark. I recorded it, hoping to catch a glimpse of my work in the background. But it wasn't in the background, it was right, slap-bang in the front-ground. The show, you see, ended with celebrity songstress Paloma Faith being invited to choose one piece of art from the entire show that she'd like to buy. And guess what she chose? I mean, seriously. Who'd have thought a puerile idea for a business card would end up in the Royal Academy and then be bought by a famous singer on prime time television? I know I didn't imagine it because I've seen the portrait hanging in Paloma Faith's bedroom. Not that I've ever visited, I hasten to add, but Paloma's bedroom was featured in a glossy interiors magazine. And there, on the wall, was my picture. I've since been offered shows by other galleries so I'm working hard to produce more art to exhibit. And all because of... you know exactly what I'm going to say, don't you... the Power of Puerility.**

SICK
BAG

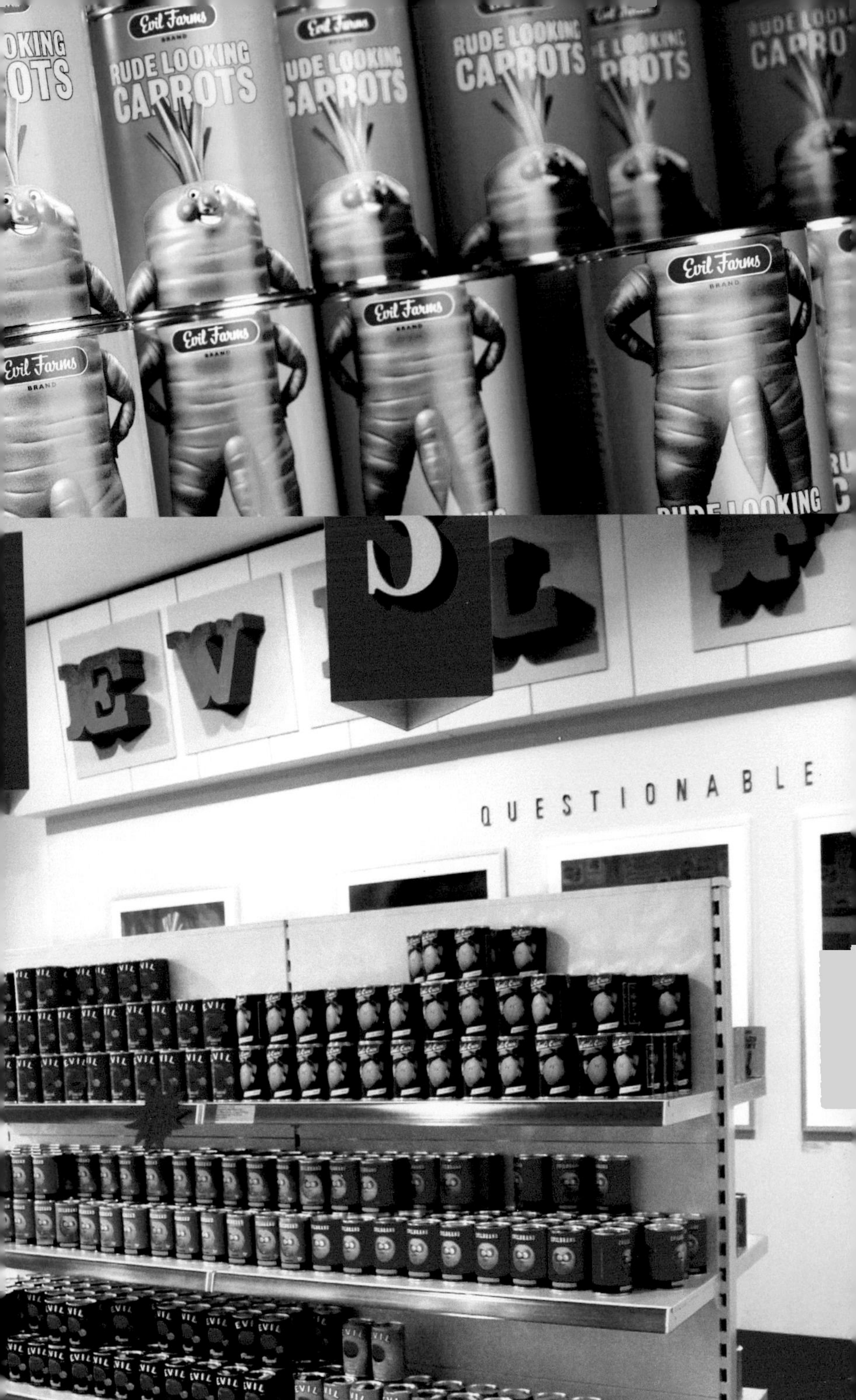
Evil Farms
BRAND
RUDE LOOKING
CARROTS
QUESTIONABLE
EVIL

EVIL
COUGH-UP
13

CASH
-44 3/4
ce-ish Day!

# OUTRODUCTION b

*an you write an outroduction for my book?'*
bsolutely I told him, then asked him what an outroduction was.
*Dunno... Dave Trott's writing the introduction...at the front...*
*thought you could write one at the back...an outroduction'.*
This exchange tells you everything you need to understand about Mark. Having known him for 25 years, I'd be pretty confident the 'outroduction' idea came about like this: 'Who's the best person in the universe to write the introduction to my book? Dave Trott! Brilliant writer, famous, got 47 million followers, AND... he's my mate. Perfect! Hang on, what about my mate Dave Dye? Not as good a writer, not as famous, only has a handful of followers, BUT...he is my mate. Fuck it! He can write the outroduction!'.
I'd put money on that. It's so Mark.
For a start, there's total disregard for convention.
(Rules, convention, the status quo, in fact all of that gang duck down the nearest alleyway whenever they see him coming their way.)
Who else, or to put it another way; who in their right mind would get a pair of jeans made out of tweed, make the Creative Circle's logo square or choose the effete Café de Paris to hold a Mexican Wrestling bout?
Then there's the childishly puerile idea; 'outroduction'.
This isn't a one off, you're holding exhibit A.
Then there's the iron will, *'I'm not accepting that I can't have what I want just because it's silly and we have no money'.*
This is a man who turns budgets of £0. into 500 page Annuals, 60 second commercials and million dollar images.
There's the humanity; 'Outroduction' Mark's ideas have an inbuilt warmth, it's impossible for him to use buzz words, I guarantee you are more likely to find the word *'dinkle'* in this book than 'data'.
Lastly, asking his mate to write something just to be nice.
He'll hate reading this schmaltzy stuff when he starts designing this book, but [redacted] and that's very rare.

Dave Dye.

Bullet Point
Pointe conique arrondie
Konische Spitze
PERMANENT MARK
Nach Gebrauch Kappe schli
★ Nur in gut belüfteten Räu
Von Kindern fernhalten.

THE
END
BIT

**I suppose I'd better wrap things up now. I hope you've enjoyed visiting my world of puerility. Oddly enough, I created this book so that I could show off all the stuff I couldn't cram into my talk. I'm now painfully aware of all the puerile pursuits that wouldn't fit into the book. Like the time I put on a World Championship Mexican wrestling event with my mate Malcolm. There was no space either for my visual obituary of the Cockney accent or the company I set up with a logo designed to scare off clients. They too, like all of my creative pursuits, opened up conversations that led to unexpected, exciting opportunities. That *is* THE POWER OF PUERILITY in action. Why not give it a bash? Give yourself permission to be stupid and propel a puerile project into the world. What have you got to lose except your reputation and a bit of moolah? Anyway, to keep up to speed with all my puerile adventures, feel free to follow me on Twitter, LinkedIn, Instagram and on the COY! blog. Better still, book me for a talk and we can meet face to face. Have fun. Your Pal, Mark Denton Esq.**

# WOW!

**Here's to the lovely people who supported this book on Kickstarter AND of course Joe Denton Esq. (my dad). I'm a little bit touched (but then again you knew that).**

Achala ODHAVJI
Adam DENTON
Adam JACKSON
Adam KING
Adam McGOWAN
Aimee LUTHER
Al YOUNG
Alan MORRICE
Alan S TRAQUAIR
Alex BAMFORD
Alex COLLEY
Alex WOOD
Andrew DAVIS
Andrew V SMITH
Anna CARPEN
Anna FAWCETT
Anna LONGARETTI
Ayoade BAMGBOYE
Bella BARR
Ben CASEY
Ben CONWAY
Ben CORFIELD
Ben GOUGH
Ben KAY
Ben MOOR
Ben PRIEST
Ben SHARPE
Benny WOOD
Billy MAWHINNEY
Bob HOFFMAN
BOYS + GIRLS
Brendan WILKINS
Brett GASCOIGNE
Brian CHAPMAN
Carl HALFORD
Carolyn DAVIS
Casey GRADY
Charles INGE
Charlie PARKER
Chris KELLY
Chris PALMER
Chris WALKER
Christopher CATCHPOLE
Claire WALLWORK
Claire WOMBWELL
Claudio PASQUALETTI
Claus LARSEN
Colin WELLS
Connor DICKSON
Constantin SARCOV
Daisie NOLAN
Dan COLE
Dan CRESTA
Dan GLOVER
Dan LACEY
Daniel HEADEY
Daniel SMITH
Danny BROOKE-TAYLOR
Danny EDWARDS
Dara LORENTZSON
Darren COMPTON-CHALK
Dave BEVERLEY
Dave DYE
Dave ROBINSON
Dave TROTT
Dave WATERS
David BILLING
David BURNS
David CONNOLLY
David GAMBLE
David GUERRERO
David MITCHELL
David SIMONS
David STEWART
Debbie CARMICHAEL
Derek SEAWARD
Diogo ABRANTES
Dolly COURSE
Dom MARTIN
Don BOWEN
Ed MORRIS
Efstathios KOUGIANOS
Elise SMIDT
Elvin PRENTICE
Emily MABEN
Enrico PAGANI
Fiona DUFFELEN
Frank HOUSTON
Franklin TIPTON
Frida LARSSON
Gareth HOWELLS
Gary WILLIS
Gordon SMITH
Graham FINK
Graham PUGH
Graham STOREY
Greg QUINTON
Guy THOMSON
Guy VICKERSTAFF
Indra SINHA
James BRADLEY
James COOK
James SEXTON
James STUDHOLM
Jamie ELLUL
Jan VAN MESDAG
Jane WHITE
Jen COMPTON-CHA
Jeremy BAKER
Jeremy GREEN
Jeremy HIBBERT
Jeremy SHARMAN
Jerry GALLAHER
Jim COMPTON-HA
Jim K DAVIES
Jo TAYLOR
Joe COLEMAN
Joe GIACOMET
John COOK
John M M FAIRLEY
John PRIEST
Johnny LEATHERS
Jon HARRISON
Jon LEVENE
Jonathan HORNER
Jonathan WILCOC